Women's Rights

Other books in the Issues on Trial Series

Women's Rights

Justin Karr, Book Editor

GREENHAVEN PRESS

An imprint of Thomson Gale, a part of The Thomson Corporation

THOMSON

GALE

Detroit • New York • San Francisco • New Haven, Conn. • Waterville, Maine • London

THOMSON
✳
™
GALE

Christine Nasso, *Publisher*
Elizabeth Des Chenes, *Managing Editor*

For more information, contact:
Greenhaven Press
27500 Drake Rd.
Farmington Hills, MI 48331-3535
Or you can visit our Internet site at http://www.gale.com

LIBRARY OF CONGRESS CATALOGING-IN-PUBLICATION DATA

Women's Rights / Justin Karr, book editor.
    p. cm. -- (Issues on trial)
  Includes bibliographical references and index.
  ISBN-13: 978-0-7377-3808-7 (hardcover)
  1. Women--Legal status, laws, etc.--United States. 2. Women's rights--United States. 3. Abortion--Law and legislation--United States. 4. Abortion--Law and legislation--United States--Cases. 5. Sex discrimination in employment--Law and legislation--United States. 6. Sex discrimination in employment--Law and legislation--United States--Cases. 7. Sex discrimination in education--Law and legislation--United States. 8. Sex discrimination in education--Law and legislation--United States--Cases. I. Karr, Justin
  KF478.W675 2008
  342.7308'78--dc22
                                                                    2007030384

ISBN-10: 0-7377-3808-1 (hardcover)

Printed in the United States of America
10 9 8 7 6 5 4 3 2 1

Contents

Chapter 1: Privacy and Freedom in Reproductive Decisions

Chapter 2: Gender Equity in the Workplace

Chapter 3: Sexual Harassment

Chapter 4: Sex Discrimination in Education

Foreword

The U.S. courts have long served as a battleground for the most highly charged and contentious issues of the time. Divisive matters are often brought into the legal system by activists who feel strongly for their cause and demand an official resolution. Indeed, subjects that give rise to intense emotions or involve closely held religious or moral beliefs lay at the heart of the most polemical court rulings in history. One such case was *Brown v. Board of Education* (1954), which ended racial segregation in schools. Prior to *Brown*, the courts had held that blacks could be forced to use separate facilities as long as these facilities were equal to that of whites.

For years many groups had opposed segregation based on religious, moral, and legal grounds. Educators produced heartfelt testimony that segregated schooling greatly disadvantaged black children. They noted that in comparison to whites, blacks received a substandard education in deplorable conditions. Religious leaders such as Martin Luther King Jr. preached that the harsh treatment of blacks was immoral and unjust. Many involved in civil rights law, such as Thurgood Marshall, called for equal protection of all people under the law, as their study of the Constitution had indicated that segregation was illegal and un-American. Whatever their motivation for ending the practice, and despite the threats they received from segregationists, these ardent activists remained unwavering in their cause.

Those fighting against the integration of schools were mainly white southerners who did not believe that whites and blacks should intermingle. Blacks were subordinate to whites, they maintained, and society had to resist any attempt to break down strict color lines. Some white southerners charged that segregated schooling was *not* hindering blacks' education. For example, Virginia attorney general J. Lindsay Almond asserted, "With the help and the sympathy and the love and respect of the white people of the South, the colored man has risen under that educational process to a place of eminence and respect throughout the nation. It has served him well." So when the Supreme Court ruled against the segregationists in *Brown*, the South responded with vociferous cries of protest. Even government leaders criticized the decision. The governor of Arkansas, Orval Faubus, stated that he would not "be a party to any attempt to force acceptance of change to which the people are so overwhelmingly opposed." Indeed, resistance to integration was so great that when black students arrived at the formerly all-white Central High School in Arkansas, federal troops had to be dispatched to quell a threatening mob of protesters.

Nevertheless, the *Brown* decision was enforced and the South integrated its schools. In this instance, the Court, while not settling the issue to everyone's satisfaction, functioned as an instrument of progress by forcing a major social change. Historian David Halberstam observes that the *Brown* ruling "deprived segregationist practices of their moral legitimacy. . . . It was therefore perhaps the single most important moment of the decade, the moment that separated the old order from the new and helped create the tumultuous era just arriving." Considered one of the most important victories for civil rights, *Brown* paved the way for challenges to racial segregation in many areas, including on public buses and in restaurants.

In examining *Brown*, it becomes apparent that the courts play an influential role—and face an arduous challenge—in shaping the debate over emotionally charged social issues. Judges must balance competing interests, keeping in mind the high stakes and intense emotions on both sides. As exemplified by *Brown*, judicial decisions often upset the status quo and initiate significant changes in society. Greenhaven Press's Issues on Trial series captures the controversy surrounding influential court rulings and explores the social ramifications of such decisions from varying perspectives. Each anthology highlights one social issue—such as the death penalty, students' rights, or wartime civil liberties. Each volume then focuses on key historical and contemporary court cases that helped mold the issue as we know it today. The books include a compendium of primary sources—court rulings, dissents, and immediate reactions to the rulings—as well as secondary sources from experts in the field, people involved in the cases, legal analysts, and other commentators opining on the implications and legacy of the chosen cases. An annotated table of contents, an in-depth introduction, and prefaces that overview each case all provide context as readers delve into the topic at hand. To help students fully probe the subject, each volume contains book and periodical bibliographies, a comprehensive index, and a list of organizations to contact. With these features, the Issues on Trial series offers a well-rounded perspective on the courts' role in framing society's thorniest, most impassioned debates.

Introduction

The past century has seen an unprecedented expansion of women's legal rights, particularly in such areas as voting, wages, protection from sexual harassment, increased educational opportunities, and the availability of birth control and legal abortion. Yet some argue that the women's rights movement has fallen victim to its own success. They contend that females born in the past few decades take for granted the rights won in the 1960s and 1970s and feel less urgency to actively protect their rights. This concerns feminists, who fear that opponents of women's rights will take advantage of this complacency and roll back hard-won gains. As humorist Erma Bombeck put it, "We've got a generation now who were born with semi-equality. They don't know how it was before, so they think, this isn't too bad. We're working. We have our attaché cases and our three piece suits. . . . They don't realize it can be taken away. Things are going to have to get worse before they join in fighting the battle."

The Court Upholds a Ban on Partial-Birth Abortion

In April 2007 the United States Supreme Court handed down a decision that embodies the concerns expressed by women's rights supporters. In *Gonzales v. Carhart*, the Court ruled 5-4 to allow enforcement of the Partial-Birth Abortion Ban Act of 2003, a federal law that prohibits a type of abortion used in the fourth through sixth months of pregnancy. Unlike previous cases, the Court approved the ban even though it contains no exception to allow the procedure when necessary to protect a woman's health—although the procedure is allowed if needed to save the woman's life. *Carhart* is the first major abortion case heard by the Supreme Court in six years. Generally, the Court has strictly limited restrictions on abortion, in keeping with the landmark *Roe v. Wade* case decided in 1973. *Roe*, the subject of Chapter 1, essentially legalized abortion in most cases until the latter third of a woman's pregnancy.

The *Carhart* decision has been applauded by anti-abortion forces and condemned by abortion-rights supporters. Both sides acknowledge that *Carhart*, on its own, may have little impact on abortion practice. The procedure it prohibits is rarely performed, and similar alternative methods will remain legal under the court's ruling. However, commentators on both sides agree that the case may pave the way for future decisions of the Court that would further restrict abortion and, perhaps, eventually overturn *Roe*, which has stood as the ultimate legal authority on abortion for over thirty years. Encouraged by the *Carhart* decision, anti-abortion members of at least a half-dozen state legislatures began work on bills to restrict abortion in their states. (Even before *Carhart*, South Dakota passed an abortion ban, although it was overturned by a public vote.) If a state were to pass a strict ban on abortion, and if the ban were challenged in court as violating the principles of *Roe*, the issue could be taken up by the U.S. Supreme Court, which would then decide whether or not to uphold *Roe*.

A Divided Supreme Court

The Supreme Court's evolving attitude toward *Roe* results from the 2006 retirement of Sandra Day O'Connor—the first female Supreme Court justice—and the recent appointment by President George W. Bush of two conservative justices, John Roberts and Samuel Alito. Roberts and Alito joined Justices Anthony Kennedy, Antonin Scalia and Clarence Thomas in forming the majority in *Carhart*. Dissenting were Justices Ruth Bader Ginsburg—the second-ever woman appointed to the court—John Paul Stevens, David Souter, and Stephen Breyer. Although much of the Court's written opinion in *Carhart* concerns the medical and legal technicalities of the abor-

tion procedure and prior court cases, both the majority and
the dissenters eventually address the moral and societal issues
involved in the abortion debate. The majority suggests that
governmental restrictions on abortion are justified in part because women may choose abortion without fully understanding the implications of the choice. Justice Kennedy, author of
the majority opinion, writes, "Respect for human life finds an
ultimate expression in the bond of love the mother has for
her child. The [Partial-Birth Abortion Ban] Act recognizes this
reality as well. Whether to have an abortion requires a difficult
and painful moral decision. While we find no reliable data to
measure the phenomenon, it seems unexceptionable to conclude some women come to regret their choice to abort the
infant life they once created and sustained. Severe depression
and loss of esteem may follow."

Justice Ginsburg, author of the dissenting opinion, suggests that the majority has simply adopted the political position of abortion opponents rather than following legal precedent. She objects to what she sees as the majority's insinuation
that women are too emotionally fragile to make difficult decisions on their own. "This way of thinking reflects ancient no-
tions about women's place in the family and under the constitution—ideas that have long since been discredited," she
writes. Just as the majority opinion encapsulates antiabortion
thought, Ginsburg's dissent echoes the arguments of abortion-
rights supporters: "In candor, the Act, and the Court's defense
of it, cannot be understood as anything other than an effort
to chip away at a right declared again and again by this
Court—and with increasing comprehension of its centrality to
women's lives."

The Potential Impact of *Gonzales v. Carhart*

Because lower courts had previously invalidated the Partial-
Birth Abortion Ban Act, it had never gone into effect. With
Carhart decided, the ban now may be enforced to outlaw the

procedure involved. The Court's opinion, however, left open the possibility that a woman actually denied an abortion under the Act could file suit if she believed enforcement of the ban was unconstitutional in her particular circumstances. Those on both sides of the abortion issue are left to wonder whether this will happen, and whether further litigation on the abortion issue will follow. The ultimate question is whether *Roe v. Wade* itself might one day be overturned, in which case states would be free to prohibit abortion entirely. It appears that at least two current justices would vote to overturn *Roe* if given the chance. In *Carhart*, Justice Thomas, in a concurring opinion joined by Justice Scalia, reiterated his belief that the Court's decision in *Roe* was unsupported by the U.S. Constitution. In any event, the *Carhart* decision has rekindled public debate over abortion. The issue likely will attract even more attention as the 2008 presidential and congressional elections near.

While abortion has been the most visible and controversial issue relating to women's rights, legislation and court cases in other areas have affected women's lives as well. Chapter 2 addresses the Equal Pay Act of 1963, which provided that women who perform the same work as men for the same employer must be paid equally. Subsequent court cases, including *Corning Glass Works v. Brennan*, decided by the U.S. Supreme Court in 1974, have further defined the right to equal pay. Meanwhile, laws such as Title VII of the Civil Rights Act of 1964 protect women from sex discrimination, particularly when it involves sexual harassment. A 1986 U.S. Supreme Court case, *Meritor Savings Bank v. Vinson*, covered in Chapter 3, extended this protection to situations involving a "hostile environment" in the workplace resulting from sexual misconduct or sexually suggestive surroundings. In another area, Title IX of the Education Amendments of 1972 prohibits schools and other organizations receiving federal funding from discriminating against females. Among the most visible changes this law has produced is a tremendous growth in female athletic programs at high schools and colleges. Chapter 4 highlights the 2005 case *Jackson v. Birmingham Board of Education*, one of many decisions that have defined the scope of Title IX over the years.

Indeed, American women have made significant legal gains in the twentieth and early twenty-first centuries. Some, including Nancy Pelosi—the first female speaker of the U.S. House of Representatives—and 2008 presidential hopeful and New York senator Hillary Rodham Clinton, have risen to positions of power in the political, legal, corporate, medical, and academic arenas. As the controversy surrounding such decisions as *Roe v. Wade* and *Gonzales v. Carhart* demonstrates, however, the country remains divided on the issue of a woman's right to abortion, due to a disagreement over the fundamental question of when life begins and the moral complexity inherent in the decision to terminate a pregnancy.

CHAPTER 1

Privacy and Freedom in Reproductive Decisions

Case Overview

Roe v. Wade (1973)

The decision in *Roe v. Wade* is one of the most significant and controversial ever handed down by the U.S. Supreme Court. The case established that a pregnant woman has a constitutional right to obtain an abortion without government interference through the first three months of pregnancy.

In 1970 attorneys for a young, unmarried, pregnant woman named Norma McCorvey sued the state of Texas alleging that a state statute banning all abortions except those necessary to save a mother's life violated the U.S. Constitution. McCorvey had agreed to be the primary plaintiff in a case to challenge the statutes, although she was referred to as "Jane Roe" to protect her identity. "Wade" was Dallas County District Attorney Henry Wade, whose office was responsible for prosecuting local violations of the statute.

Before the case reached the Supreme Court, Roe's lawyers argued to the Fifth U.S. Circuit Court of Appeals that the Texas abortion statute deprived Roe of her constitutional privacy rights. Attorneys for the state contended that the state was entitled to ban abortion on the grounds that an unborn child's right to life was more important than the mother's right to privacy. The three-judge panel sided with Roe, ruling that the statute was unconstitutional. However, because the circuit court did not order Texas to cease enforcement of the statute, Roe was entitled to appeal the case to the Supreme Court.

The Supreme Court ruled 7-2 that the Texas statute violated the U.S. Constitution. The Court found that the right to privacy established by the 1965 *Griswold v. Connecticut* case involving contraceptives was broad enough to encompass a woman's decision to terminate her pregnancy, with some limitations. The Court reasoned that state abortion laws were no longer necessary to protect a woman's health during the procedure because advances in technology had made abortion safer than childbirth. At the same time the Court concluded that the definition of "persons" in the Constitution does not include fetuses, which would have required greater governmental protection. *Roe* established a legal framework based on the three trimesters (roughly three-month periods) of pregnancy. During the first trimester, abortion was to be unregulated by law. During the second trimester, states could regulate abortion as necessary to protect a woman's health. During the third trimester, after the fetus is deemed viable, or able to survive outside the womb, states would be permitted to regulate or restrict abortion except when necessary to preserve a woman's life.

In the years since *Roe v. Wade* was decided, the case has created a bitter divide between "pro-choice" advocates, who believe the decision to legally end an unwanted pregnancy is a fundamental right, and "pro-life" advocates, who believe that destroying a fetus is tantamount to murder. Ironically, the plaintiff, Norma McCorvey, initially became a spokesperson for pro-choice organizations then later had a change of heart and became a prominent pro-life activist. The issue of abortion has been contested in numerous Supreme Court cases since 1973. The Court has distanced itself somewhat from the trimester framework and has upheld various governmental regulations and restrictions on abortion. However, it has held to the view that abortion is a basic human right and that abortion restrictions should never place an "undue burden" on women.

> *"This right of privacy . . . is broad enough to encompass a woman's decision whether or not to terminate her pregnancy."*

The Court's Decision: State Criminal Abortion Laws Violate a Woman's Right to Privacy

Justice Harry Blackmun

Justice Harry A. Blackmun was born in Nashville, Illinois, in 1908. He received degrees from Harvard University and Harvard Law School. Justice Blackmun worked in private practice in Minneapolis, Minnesota, from 1934 to 1950, during which time he also served on the adjunct faculty at the University of Minnesota Law School and the St. Paul College of Law. In 1959 President Dwight D. Eisenhower appointed Blackmun to the United States Court of Appeals for the Eighth Circuit. He was appointed to the U.S. Supreme Court in 1970 by President Richard M. Nixon. Justice Blackmun served on the Court until June 30, 1994, and died in 1999 at the age of ninety.

The U.S. Supreme Court's 1973 decision in the abortion-rights case of Roe v. Wade *is one of the most far-reaching and controversial rulings ever handed down by the Court. The following piece is an excerpt from the majority opinion in* Roe *authored by Justice Blackmun. The Supreme Court declared that state governments may not prohibit a woman from obtaining an abortion in the first six months of pregnancy, although some restrictions may be imposed. The Court further ruled that in the*

Justice Harry Blackmun, majority opinion, *Roe v. Wade*, 410 U.S. 113, 1973.

final three months of pregnancy, states may further restrict and even prohibit abortion, except when an abortion is necessary to save the health or life of the mother.

The Constitution does not explicitly mention any right of privacy. In a line of decisions, however, going back perhaps as far as *Union Pacific R. Co. v. Botsford* (1891), the Court has recognized that a right of personal privacy, or a guarantee of certain areas or zones of privacy, does exist under the Constitution. In varying contexts, the Court or individual Justices have, indeed, found at least the roots of that right in the First Amendment, in the penumbras of the Bill of Rights, in the Ninth Amendment, or in the concept of liberty guaranteed by the first section of the Fourteenth Amendment. [Case citations omitted throughout.] These decisions make it clear that only personal rights that can be deemed "fundamental" or "implicit in the concept of ordered liberty," are included in this guarantee of personal privacy. They also make it clear that the right has some extension to activities relating to marriage, procreation, contraception, family relationships, and child rearing and education.

Detriments of Denying Choice

This right of privacy, whether it be founded in the Fourteenth Amendment's concept of personal liberty and restrictions upon state action, as we feel it is, or, as the District Court determined, in the Ninth Amendment's reservation of rights to the people, is broad enough to encompass a woman's decision whether or not to terminate her pregnancy. The detriment that the State would impose upon the pregnant woman by denying this choice altogether is apparent. Specific and direct harm medically diagnosable even in early pregnancy may be involved. Maternity, or additional offspring, may force upon the woman a distressful life and future. Psychological harm may be imminent. Mental and physical health may be taxed by child care. There is also the distress, for all concerned, associated with the unwanted child, and there is the problem of bringing a child into a family already unable, psychologically and otherwise, to care for it. In other cases, as in this one, the additional difficulties and continuing stigma of unwed motherhood may be involved. All these are factors the woman and her responsible physician necessarily will consider in consultation.

On the basis of elements such as these, appellant and some amici [organizations supporting *Roe*'s legal position] argue that the woman's right is absolute and that she is entitled to terminate her pregnancy at whatever time, in whatever way, and for whatever reason she alone chooses. With this we do not agree. Appellant's arguments that Texas either has no valid interest at all in regulating the abortion decision, or no interest strong enough to support any limitation upon the woman's sole determination, are unpersuasive. The Court's decisions recognizing a right of privacy also acknowledge that some state regulation in areas protected by that right is appropriate. As noted above, a State may properly assert important interests in safeguarding health, in maintaining medical standards, and in protecting potential life. At some point in pregnancy, these respective interests become sufficiently compelling to sustain regulation of the factors that govern the abortion decision. The privacy right involved, therefore, cannot be said to be absolute. In fact, it is not clear to us that the claim asserted by some amici that one has an unlimited right to do with one's body as one pleases bears a close relationship to the right of privacy previously articulated in the Court's decisions. The Court has refused to recognize an unlimited right of this kind in the past.

Abortion Right Has Limitations

We, therefore, conclude that the right of personal privacy includes the abortion decision, but that this right is not unqualified and must be considered against important state interests in regulation.

We note that those federal and state courts that have recently considered abortion law challenges have reached the same conclusion. A majority, in addition to the District Court in the present case, have held state laws unconstitutional, at least in part, because of vagueness or because of overbreadth and abridgment of rights.

Others have sustained state statutes.

Although the results are divided, most of these courts have agreed that the right of privacy, however based, is broad enough to cover the abortion decision; that the right, nonetheless, is not absolute and is subject to some limitations; and that at some point the state interests as to protection of health, medical standards, and prenatal life, become dominant. We agree with this approach.

Regulation Must Be Justified

Where certain "fundamental rights" are involved, the Court has held that regulation limiting these rights may be justified only by a "compelling state interest" and that legislative enactments must be narrowly drawn to express only the legitimate state interests at stake.

In the recent abortion cases, cited above, courts have recognized these principles. Those striking down state laws have generally scrutinized the State's interests in protecting health and potential life, and have concluded that neither interest justified broad limitations on the reasons for which a physician and his pregnant patient might decide that she should have an abortion in the early stages of pregnancy. Courts sustaining state laws have held that the State's determinations to protect health or prenatal life are dominant and constitutionally justifiable.

Balancing Interests

The District Court held that the appellee failed to meet his burden of demonstrating that the Texas statute's infringement upon Roe's rights was necessary to support a compelling state interest, and that, although the appellee presented "several compelling justifications for state presence in the area of abortions," the statutes outstripped these justifications and swept "far beyond any areas of compelling state interest." Appellant and appellee both contest that holding. Appellant, as has been indicated, claims an absolute right that bars any state imposition of criminal penalties in the area. Appellee argues that the State's determination to recognize and protect prenatal life from and after conception constitutes a compelling state interest. As noted above, we do not agree fully with either formulation.

The appellee and certain amici argue that the fetus is a "person" within the language and meaning of the Fourteenth Amendment. In support of this, they outline at length and in detail the well-known facts of fetal development. If this suggestion of personhood is established, the appellant's case, of course, collapses, for the fetus' right to life would then be guaranteed specifically by the Amendment. The appellant conceded as much on reargument. On the other hand, the appellee conceded on reargument that no case could be cited that holds that a fetus is a person within the meaning of the Fourteenth Amendment.

Is the Fetus a "Person?"

The Constitution does not define "person" in so many words. Section 1 of the Fourteenth Amendment contains three references to "person." The first, in defining "citizens," speaks of "persons born or naturalized in the United States." The word also appears both in the Due Process Clause and in the Equal Protection Clause. "Person" is used in other places in the Constitution: in the listing of qualifications for Representatives and Senators, in the Apportionment Clause, in the Migration and Importation provision, in the Emolument Clause, in the Electors provisions, in the provision outlining qualifications for the office of President, in the Extradition provisions, and in the Fifth, Twelfth, and Twenty-second Amendments, as well as in 2 and 3 of the Fourteenth Amendment. But in nearly all these instances, the use of the word is such that it has application only postnatally. None indicates, with any assurance, that it has any possible pre-natal application.

All this, together with our observation [above] that throughout the major portion of the 19th century prevailing legal abortion practices were far freer than they are today, persuades us that the word "person," as used in the Fourteenth Amendment, does not include the unborn. This is in accord with the results reached in those few cases where the issue has been squarely presented. Indeed, our decision in *United States v. Vuitch* inferentially is to the same effect, for we there would not have indulged in statutory interpretation favorable to abortion in specified circumstances if the necessary consequence was the termination of life entitled to Fourteenth Amendment protection.

Additional Considerations

This conclusion, however, does not of itself fully answer the contentions raised by Texas, and we pass on to other considerations.

The pregnant woman cannot be isolated in her privacy. She carries an embryo and, later, a fetus, if one accepts the medical definitions of the developing young in the human uterus. The situation therefore is inherently different from marital intimacy, or bedroom possession of obscene material, or marriage, or procreation, or education, with which [other decisions of this Court] were respectively concerned. As we have intimated above, it is reasonable and appropriate for a State to decide that at some point in time another interest, that of health of the mother or that of potential human life, becomes significantly involved. The woman's privacy is no longer sole and any right of privacy she possesses must be measured accordingly.

When Life Begins Not Decided

Texas urges that, apart from the Fourteenth Amendment, life begins at conception and is present throughout pregnancy, and that, therefore, the State has a compelling interest in protecting that life from and after conception. We need not resolve the difficult question of when life begins. When those trained in the respective disciplines of medicine, philosophy, and theology are unable to arrive at any consensus, the judiciary, at this point in the development of man's knowledge, is not in a position to speculate as to the answer.

It should be sufficient to note briefly the wide divergence of thinking on this most sensitive and difficult question. There has always been strong support for the view that life does not begin until live birth. This was the belief of the Stoics. It appears to be the predominant, though not the unanimous, attitude of the Jewish faith. It may be taken to represent also the position of a large segment of the Protestant community, insofar as that can be ascertained; organized groups that have taken a formal position on the abortion issue have generally regarded abortion as a matter for the conscience of the individual and her family. As we have noted, the common law found greater significance in quickening. Physicians and their scientific colleagues have regarded that event with less interest and have tended to focus either upon conception, upon live birth, or upon the interim point at which the fetus becomes "viable," that is, potentially able to live outside the mother's womb, albeit with artificial aid. Viability is usually placed at about seven months (28 weeks) but may occur earlier, even at 24 weeks. The Aristotelian theory of "mediate animation," that held sway throughout the Middle Ages and the Renaissance in

Europe, continued to be official Roman Catholic dogma until the 19th century, despite opposition to this "ensoulment" theory from those in the Church who would recognize the existence of life from the moment of conception. The latter is now, of course, the official belief of the Catholic Church. As one brief amicus [legal brief from a supporting organization] discloses, this is a view strongly held by many non-Catholics as well, and by many physicians. Substantial problems for precise definition of this view are posed, however, by new embryological data that purport to indicate that conception is a "process" over time, rather than an event, and by new medical techniques such as menstrual extraction, the "morning-after" pill, implantation of embryos, artificial insemination, and even artificial wombs.

Rights of the Unborn Restricted

In areas other than criminal abortion, the law has been reluctant to endorse any theory that life, as we recognize it, begins before live birth or to accord legal rights to the unborn except in narrowly defined situations and except when the rights are contingent upon live birth. For example, the traditional rule of tort law denied recovery for prenatal injuries even though the child was born alive. That rule has been changed in almost every jurisdiction. In most States, recovery is said to be permitted only if the fetus was viable, or at least quick, when the injuries were sustained, though few courts have squarely so held. In a recent development, generally opposed by the commentators, some States permit the parents of a stillborn child to maintain an action for wrongful death because of prenatal injuries. Such an action, however, would appear to be one to vindicate the parents' interest and is thus consistent with the view that the fetus, at most, represents only the potentiality of life. Similarly, unborn children have been recognized as acquiring rights or interests by way of inheritance or other devolution of property, and have been represented by guardians ad litem [court-appointed representatives who protect children's legal rights]. Perfection of the interests involved, again, has generally been contingent upon live birth. In short, the unborn have never been recognized in the law as persons in the whole sense.

In view of all this, we do not agree that, by adopting one theory of life, Texas may override the rights of the pregnant woman that are at stake. We repeat, however, that the State does have an important and legitimate interest in preserving and protecting the health of the pregnant woman, whether she be a resident of the State or a nonresident who seeks medical consultation and treatment there, and that it has still another important and legitimate interest in protecting the potentiality of human life. These interests are separate and distinct. Each grows in substantiality as the woman approaches term and, at a point during pregnancy, each becomes "compelling."

Importance of First Trimester

With respect to the State's important and legitimate interest in the health of the mother, the "compelling" point, in the light of present medical knowledge, is at approximately the end of the first trimester [first three months of pregnancy]. This is so because of the now-established medical fact, that until the end of the first trimester mortality in abortion may be less than mortality in normal childbirth. It follows that, from and after this point, a State may regulate the abortion procedure to the extent that the regulation reasonably relates to the preservation and protection of maternal health. Examples of permissible state regulation in this area are requirements as to the qualifications of the person who is to perform the abortion; as to the licensure of that person; as to the facility in which the procedure is to be performed, that is, whether it must be a hospital or may be a clinic or some other place of less-than-hospital status; as to the licensing of the facility; and the like.

This means, on the other hand, that, for the period of pregnancy prior to this "compelling" point, the attending physician, in consultation with his patient, is free to determine, without regulation by the State, that, in his medical judgment, the patient's pregnancy should be terminated. If that decision is reached, the judgment may be effectuated by an abortion free of interference by the State.

Late Abortion Prohibited

With respect to the State's important and legitimate interest in potential life, the "compelling" point is at viability. This is so because the fetus then presumably has the capability of meaningful life outside the mother's womb. State regulation protective of fetal life after viability thus has both logical and biological justifications. If the State is interested in protecting fetal life after viability, it may go so far as to proscribe abortion during that period, except when it is necessary to preserve the life or health of the mother.

Measured against these standards, Art. 1196 of the Texas Penal Code, in restricting legal abortions to those "procured or attempted by medical advice for the purpose of saving the life of the mother," sweeps too broadly. The statute makes no distinction between abortions performed early in pregnancy and those performed later, and it limits to a single reason, "saving" the mother's life, the legal justification for the procedure. The statute, therefore, cannot survive the constitutional attack made upon it here.

> *"The Court apparently values the convenience of the pregnant mother more than the continued existence and development of the life or potential life that she carries."*

Dissenting Opinion: The Constitution Does Not Guarantee the Right to an Abortion

Justice Byron White

Justice Byron R. White was a Rhodes Scholar and a former NFL (National Football League) player. He was appointed to the U.S. Supreme Court by President John F. Kennedy in 1962 and served for thirty-one years. During his time on the Court, Justice White was considered a judicial conservative, dissenting in the abortion-rights cases Doe v. Bolton *and* Roe v. Wade. *He died in 2002 at the age of eighty-four.*

The following essay is an excerpt from the dissenting opinion in Roe v. Wade. *Justice White, joined here in dissent by Justice William Rehnquist, asserts that nothing in the language or history of the U.S. Constitution supports the reasoning upon which the majority rests its opinion. In White's view, the states should be allowed to weigh the interests of the pregnant woman against those of the fetus and regulate or prohibit abortion at any time during pregnancy.*

Justice Byron White, dissenting opinion, *Roe v. Wade*, 410 U.S. 113, 1973.

At the heart of the controversy in these cases are those recurring pregnancies that pose no danger whatsoever to the life or health of the mother but are, nevertheless, unwanted for any one or more of a variety of reasons—convenience, family planning, economics, dislike of children, the embarrassment of illegitimacy, etc. The common claim before us is that, for any one of such reasons, or for no reason at all, and without asserting or claiming any threat to life or health, any woman is entitled to an abortion at her request if she is able to find a medical advisor willing to undertake the procedure.

The Court, for the most part, sustains this position: during the period prior to the time the fetus becomes viable, the Constitution of the United States values the convenience, whim, or caprice of the putative mother more than the life or potential life of the fetus: the Constitution, therefore, guarantees the right to an abortion as against any state law or policy seeking to protect the fetus from an abortion not prompted by more compelling reasons of the mother.

No Historical Support

With all due respect, I dissent. I find nothing in the language or history of the Constitution to support the Court's judgment. The Court simply fashions and announces a new constitutional right for pregnant mothers and, with scarcely any reason or authority for its action, invests that right with sufficient substance to override most existing state abortion statutes. The upshot is that the people and the legislatures of the 50 States are constitutionally disentitled to weigh the relative importance of the continued existence and development of the fetus, on the one hand, against a spectrum of possible impacts on the mother, on the other hand. As an exercise of raw judicial power, the Court perhaps has authority to do what it does today; but, in my view, its judgment is an improvident and extravagant exercise of the power of judicial review that the Constitution extends to this Court.

The Court apparently values the convenience of the pregnant mother more than the continued existence and development of the life or potential life that she carries. Whether or not I might agree with that marshaling of values, I can in no event join the Court's judgment because I find no constitutional warrant for imposing such an order of priorities on the people and legislatures of the States. In a sensitive area such as this, involving as it does issues over which reasonable men may easily and heatedly differ, I cannot accept the Court's exercise of its clear power of choice by interposing a constitutional barrier to state efforts to protect human life and by investing mothers and doctors with the constitutionally protected right to exterminate it. This issue, for the most part, should be left with the people and to the political processes the people have devised to govern their affairs.

Uphold State Laws

It is my view, therefore, that the Texas statute is not constitutionally infirm because it denies abortions to those who seek to serve only their convenience, rather than to protect their life or health. Nor is this plaintiff, who claims no threat to her mental or physical health, entitled to assert the possible rights of those women whose pregnancy assertedly implicates their health. This, together with *United States v. Vuitch*, (1971), dictates reversal of the judgment of the District Court.

Likewise, because Georgia may constitutionally forbid abortions to putative mothers who, like the plaintiff in this case, do not fall within the reach of § 26-1202(a) of its criminal code. I have no occasion, and the District Court had none, to consider the constitutionality of the procedural requirements of the Georgia statute as applied to those pregnancies posing substantial hazards to either life or health. I would reverse the judgment of the District Court in the Georgia case.

"One can feel bad, sorry, or regretful that any woman ever has an unwanted pregnancy. One can also feel truly wonderful that safe abortions are legally available when wanted.' These are not contradictory positions."

A Moral Defense of Abortion

Caitlin Borgmann and Catherine Weiss

At the time this essay was originally published, Caitlin Borgmann held the position of state strategies coordinator for the American Civil Liberties Union Reproductive Freedom Project in New York, and Catherine Weiss served as its director.

In the following selection, Borgmann and Weiss note that young women growing up in the three decades after the historic Roe v. Wade *decision have never known a world of illegal, unsafe abortions. The authors contend that because many females take for granted the right to terminate pregnancy, pro-life activists have been able to gain momentum in their efforts to restrict reproductive freedom and perhaps overturn* Roe v. Wade.

The movement to preserve and advance reproductive freedom is suffering the consequences of a great victory. The establishment of the constitutional right to abortion in *Roe v. Wade* was a monumental step that changed the lives of American women. Girls grow up today under the mantle of *Roe*, never having known a world in which illegal, unsafe, degrad-

Caitlin Borgmann and Catherine Weiss, "Beyond Apocalypse and Apology: A Moral Defense of Abortion," *Perspectives on Sexual and Reproductive Health*, vol. 35, no. 1, January-February 2003, pp. 40–43. Copyright © 2003 Alan Guttmacher Institute. Reproduced by permission of Alan Guttmacher Institute.

ing and sometimes fatal abortions were the norm. That is a cause for celebration as *Roe* turns 30. It is also, however, a cause of complacency. Movements typically subside after winning major legal or political battles, and ours has not escaped this cycle.

Complacency corrodes all freedoms. It is particularly dangerous to reproductive freedom because our opponents are single-minded and fervent to the point of fanaticism. Their crusade has fueled three decades of incremental restrictions that make it risky or burdensome to get an abortion and, for some women, block access altogether. Understandably, the prochoice movement has grown frustrated with the unending onslaught, and the public, numb. The movement's responses to this conundrum have varied over time and among its many spokespersons. Yet, two recurring approaches—to jolt the public by forecasting *Roe's* reversal and to court reluctant supporters by steering wide of abortion altogether—are problematic. We need to recapture at least some of the moral urgency that led to *Roe*, and we must meet the assaults head-on.

Freedom Threatened

Reproductive freedom is in trouble. The Supreme Court has refrained from overturning *Roe* but has allowed the states to layer myriad restrictions on abortion. The states, seizing the opportunity to regulate women's lives, enacted more than 300 restrictions on access to abortion and other reproductive health services between 1995 and 2001. Some of the most common laws affect all women seeking abortions in a particular state: For example, 18 states require counseling designed to dissuade women from having abortions, followed by a waiting period before an abortion can be performed.

The assault on *Roe* has done the most damage, however, to women whose voices are largely ignored in the political debate and whose interests carry the least political weight. Low-income women face what can be prohibitive costs in seeking abortions. Very few have private health insurance, and government-supported plans rarely pay for abortions. Moreover, these women face significant financial obstacles merely to get to a provider. Nationwide, 87% of all counties lack abortion providers (because of inadequate training opportunities for medical students, burdensome regulations targeted at abortion providers, and a climate of harassment and violence, among other factors). For low-income women living in rural areas, this can mean adding costs for travel, time away from jobs and child care to the cost of the abortion itself.

Teenagers Bear Burden

Teenagers have also suffered the brunt of abortion restrictions. More than half the states enforce laws that deny those younger than 18 access to a legal abortion unless they involve a parent or go to court. Teenagers who consult their parents under compulsion of the law and against their better judgment often find their fears justified: They are kicked out of their homes, beaten and prevented from obtaining abortions. The alternative of going to court is daunting for any teenager, and especially for one who is pregnant, desperate and unsupported by her family. Often, she must explain multiple absences from school without raising suspicions, find a lawyer who will help her, brave one or more trips to the courthouse, tell the intimate details of her personal life to numerous strangers and then hope that the judge grants her the permission she needs.

Yet, advocates for reproductive freedom tire of talking about these restrictions, and few people seem interested in hearing about them. Because most middle-class, adult women can get abortions in spite of the prevalent restrictions, the majoritarian passion to preserve the right established in *Roe* has faded, leaving the most vulnerable women isolated and powerless. They have reason to wonder what we are celebrating at *Roe's* anniversary.

What we need to celebrate is renewed unity, commitment, energy and purpose. Unfortunately, the movement has sometimes tried to achieve these by either dwelling on the possibility that abortion will again be illegal or minimizing the importance of abortion. We refer to these two tendencies as the apocalyptic and the apologetic approaches.

The Apocalyptic Approach

The apocalyptic approach aims to rouse the public from complacency by positing an immediate and personal threat: Women will no longer be able to get an abortion when they need one. This approach recognizes that a woman who thinks that the abortion rights battle is over and won can be goaded into action if she is convinced that the victory is about to be reversed and that its reversal will affect her. The threat posed must be imminent, real and personal.

Typically, the apocalyptic approach warns that the Supreme Court is on the brink of overturning *Roe v. Wade*. To emphasize the immediacy of the threat, this approach highlights the hostility of the current administration and the advancing age of several justices who support women's right to choose. Focusing on the worst-case scenario—the Court's complete overturning of *Roe*—makes the threat personal to a broad swath of Americans. Thus, this approach hopes to draw in people who are not moved to activism in opposition to narrower restrictions.

New Attack on *Roe*

There can be no doubt that the already battered right declared in *Roe* faces new and powerful assaults. Both the White House and the Congress are enemies of choice and stand prepared to appoint and confirm like-minded judges—not only to the Supreme Court, but also to the lower federal courts where most abortion rights cases are decided. In addition, Congress is now in a position to pass long-threatened federal restrictions, posing yet more obstacles to abortion nationwide.

The question remains, however, whether these assaults will prove fatal to *Roe* itself. If history is any guide, the Supreme Court may well continue to say that *Roe* is good law while upholding one restriction after another. This is the compromise the Court adopted in the late 1980s and openly embraced in its 1992 decision in *Planned Parenthood v. Casey*. The Court there proclaimed, "the essential holding of *Roe v. Wade* should be retained and once again reaffirmed," but then added, "the fact that a law ... has the incidental effect of making it more difficult or more expensive to procure an abortion cannot be enough to invalidate it" If the Court follows this pattern, the damage, while devastating, will continue to be incremental, cumulative and obscure, rather than dramatic, sudden and obvious. Of course, the harms will accumulate faster as the courts grow more hostile.

Ignoring Threat Is Risky

Because a candid reversal of *Roe* is neither certain nor immediate, people may react to constant warnings as they would to a car alarm that goes off at all hours—it is annoying, but they learn to ignore it. We risk being unable to galvanize the public if and when we confront the imminent possibility of *Roe's* demise.

Moreover, constantly referring to the possibility of losing the "core right" to abortion diverts attention from the significant encroachments that have already been and continue to be placed on the right. Under this approach, whether the core right exists is effectively measured by whether a middle-class, adult woman has access to an abortion. Meanwhile, a low-income woman has, for all intents and purposes, already lost her core right if she depends on Medicaid for her medical care but is denied coverage for an abortion; if she lives in a rural state with no abortion provider within 200 miles; and if she must make two trips to that distant provider, thanks to a state-imposed waiting period. Her right is a hollow promise when the government is permitted to erect so many hurdles that they create an impasse.

The Apologetic Approach

The apologetic approach takes a different attack. Reacting to a widespread and apparently growing discomfort with abortion, it focuses predominantly on topics the public finds more palatable, such as contraception and sexuality education. It minimizes discussion of abortion, or characterizes abortion as regrettably necessary.

This approach hopes to garner additional supporters for the movement's overall agenda by beginning with more popular subjects. Unfortunately, it does not always proceed from there. Bringing people into the fold by first discussing different (though related) issues may create an opening to convince them about the importance of access to abortion, but it is not a substitute.

Addressing Public Uncertainty

The apologetic approach also hopes to draw people in by identifying with their misgivings about abortion. Respect for uncertainties and objections is critical to any conversation about deeply held values, but the apologetic approach does not engage in moral dialogue. Instead, it mirrors the public's general skittishness about abortion.

The tendency to shy from open discussion of and support for abortion plays into the hands of our opponents. They want the public to associate abortion with secrecy, trauma, stigma, guilt, fear and shame. Both our silence and our apologies reinforce these associations, however unintentionally. Our opponents say that abortion is murder, we imply or say that it is regrettable, and the public slides further into ambivalence. Recent polling data suggest such slippage in public support.

Not Guilty of Extremism

Furthermore, the apologetic approach tacitly promotes the myth that the prochoice movement is too extreme. This approach calls for putting on a fresh and friendly face, to contrast with the glare of the stereotypical radical feminist. But we have not been frowning on childbearing, fighting for abortion on demand until moments before birth or generally scorning the views of the public. We do not need to pursue moderation as though we have been guilty of extremism.

When we smile brightly and sidestep the issue of abortion, we risk alienating our strongest supporters. They understand that abortion rights are part of a larger constellation of both rights and aspirations. We stand not only for the right to choose, but also for comprehensive sexuality education, effective contraceptive options, quality prenatal care and childbirth assistance, and trustworthy and affordable child care. Focusing on abortion to the exclusion of all else is a mistake—but so is avoiding the subject of abortion. When we are evasive, our supporters may doubt our commitment, even if they understand that our evasiveness reflects a tactical strategy rather than a shift in principle. They may wonder about the effectiveness of outreach efforts that omit or equivocate about so important a topic and, thus, forgo the opportunity to educate people about the ongoing, cumulative damage to abortion rights.

A Solution Among Limited Options

In its hesitance to defend abortion, the apologetic approach shrinks from the wrong demon. It is an unwanted or unhealthy pregnancy that causes a woman to confront the abortion decision. Once she is in this predicament, abortion may be a welcome solution among very limited options. Bemoaning abortion is like lamenting open-heart surgery in the face of Americans' unacceptably high rate of heart disease. We hope never to need a coronary bypass, but we are grateful to have the procedure available if we need it. Similarly, as critics of the apologetic approach have pointed out, "One can feel bad, sorry, or regretful that any woman ever has an unwanted pregnancy. One can also feel truly wonderful that safe abortions are legally available when wanted." [Quoting Alstad, D. and Kramer, J., Abortion and the Morality Wars: Taking the Moral Offensive, www.rit.org/editorials/abortion/moralwar.html, accessed December 3, 2002.] These are not contradictory positions.

Abortion as a Moral Choice

An alternative to the apocalyptic and apologetic approaches is a realistic, direct defense that recalls the reasons we fought for legal abortion in the first place. It argues forcefully to a generation that expects equality that without the right to decide whether to continue a pregnancy, a woman's autonomy and equality are compromised. It documents the critical role that access to abortion has played in women's lives over the past 30 years. Rather than focusing on whether we are about to lose *Roe* altogether, it exposes, defends against and attempts to reverse the constant whittling away that diminishes the right to abortion every year. It focuses attention on the unfairness of laws that in effect deny this right to the most vulnerable women.

To defend abortion with confidence, we must first recognize that institutional opposition to the right is part of a broader campaign to undermine women's autonomy and equality. Antichoice leaders see sexuality (especially women's) divorced from procreation as shameful, women as inadequate to make weighty moral decisions and forced childbearing as appropriate punishment for sexual irresponsibility. They approve of requiring women to pay out of pocket for contraception, while ensuring that insurance plans cover men's access to Viagra; reducing sexuality education to a "just say no" mantra and consigning those teenagers who say yes to the deadly risks of unprotected sex; and denying poor women the means to obtain abortions, yet refusing to help them provide adequate food, shelter and education for the children they bear. Abortion is only one piece of the puzzle.

Contradictory Positions

When this puzzle is assembled, the image that emerges is of a woman subjugated, not a fetus saved. For example, it is illuminating that "right-to-life" leaders generally tolerate abortion in cases of rape or incest. The fetus conceived by rape is biologically and morally indistinguishable from the fetus conceived by voluntary intercourse. But in the view of our opponents, the rape victim is innocent while the woman who chooses to have sex is tainted. For them, it is the woman's innocence or guilt that determines whether she should be allowed to have an abortion or forced to bear a child.

The impulse to punish women rather than to help children is equally evident in the policies of antichoice states with regard to children already born. If the motivation behind abortion restrictions were really the love of babies, antichoice states should have child-friendly laws. Yet the opposite is so. A comprehensive review of the abortion and child welfare policies in the 50 states demonstrates that the states with the most restrictive abortion laws also spend the least to facilitate adoption, to provide subsistence to poor children and to educate children in general. The study concludes, "Pro-life states are less likely than pro-choice states to provide adequate care to poor and needy children. Their concern for the weak and vulnerable appears to stop at birth." The seemingly contradictory coexistence of "pro-life" laws and antichild policies is explained, in significant part, by opposition to women's changing roles in society: The more hostile statewide public opinion is toward women's equality and the lower women's income is relative to men's, the more likely the state is both to restrict abortion and to impoverish children.

In contrast, our position is prowoman, profamily, prochild and prochoice. This is a moral debate we must have and can win. Such a debate can move doubters to become moral defenders of a woman's decision to have an abortion. Even those who remain personally opposed to abortion may come to support each woman's right to make the decision in accordance with her own conscience, commitments and beliefs. What follows are some of the best reasons to support abortion rights.

Autonomy of Women

A woman deciding whether to continue a pregnancy stands on moral ground. She is entitled to make her decision, and she must live with the consequences. No one else—and certainly not the government—should decide whether she will use her body to bring new life into the world. The decision is too intimate and too important to be taken from her.

In everyday life, men and women make decisions that affect the life and death of existing people. They decide whether to join the army; whether to donate blood, a kidney or bone marrow to a child; whether to give money to Save the Children instead of buying a new sweater, whether to decline a lifesaving blood transfusion; whether to drive a small fort on wheels that may protect its passengers in a crash but often kills those in less-substantial vehicles. Few question adults' autonomy to make these decisions, although some may criticize the individual choice made.

Yet, our opponents want a different standard to govern women's decisions about abortion. They portray women who demand the right to make this decision as selfish and immoral, although even many "prolifers" place fetuses on a lower moral plane than existing people (hence their tolerance of abortion in cases of rape and incest, among other inconsistencies). In response, we must staunchly defend women's ability and right to be moral actors, especially when they are making decisions about reproduction.

Equality for Women

Without the right of reproductive choice, women cannot participate equally in the nation's social, political and economic life. Their freedom to decide whether and when to have children opens doors that would otherwise be closed. They may learn to be electricians, librarians, roofers, teachers or triathletes; care for their young children or aging parents; start and finish college; wait until they are financially and emotionally prepared to support a child; keep a steady job; marry if and when they want to.

Women still do the bulk of the work of raising children and caring for extended families. Whether they experience this work as a privilege, a necessity, a burden or all three, increasing their control over the scope and timing of these responsibilities can only help them to secure a more equal footing on whatever paths they travel. In fact, in countries throughout the world, women's desire and ability to limit the number of children they have go hand in hand with their educational advancement and economic independence.

Bodily Integrity of Women

Women should have control over their own bodies. In virtually all other contexts, the law treats a person's body as inviolable. Prisoners are denied many of their most important personal liberties, yet are protected from unreasonable invasions of their bodies (such as routine body cavity searches). Similarly, the state cannot require a crime victim to undergo an operation to recover evidence (such as a bullet), even if that evidence would help to convict a murder suspect. And no law can force an unwilling parent to undergo bodily invasions far less risky than pregnancy (such as donating bone marrow) to save a living child. "It is difficult to imagine a clearer case of bodily intrusion" than for the government to demand that a woman continue a pregnancy and go through childbirth against her will.

Wantedness and Welcome

The decision to have a child—even more than the decision to have an abortion—carries profound moral implications. Unless a woman is willing to bear a child and give it up for adoption, she should have children when she feels she can welcome them. A mother's freedom to decide whether and when to have an additional child contributes immeasurably to the welfare of the children she already has, as well as any yet to be born. A teenager's decision to delay having a child until a time when she can provide adequate financial and emotional support increases the probability that when she does decide to have a family, it will be healthy and stable. Indeed, many women who decide not to have a child at a particular time do so out of reverence for children.

Personal and Public Health

Finally, the right to abortion promotes personal and public health. We know that criminal bans do not stop women from seeking abortions. The desperate measures women in pre-*Roe* days felt driven to take to terminate their unwanted pregnancies are testament to how untenable the prospect of childbearing can be. Access to safe, legal abortion ensures that women will not be maimed or killed when they decide they cannot continue a pregnancy. Similarly, access to safe abortion ensures that women can terminate pregnancies that endanger their health. A pregnant woman with a heart condition, uncontrolled hypertension, diabetes or one of a host of other problems must have all medically accepted options open to her. She, her loved ones and her doctor must be able to respond to shifting and serious health risks without having to consult a lawyer.

These reasons to support abortion rights are not new. All of them predate *Roe v. Wade*, some by centuries. Yet, as *Roe* turns 30 and continues its embattled advance toward middle age, these reasons are as pressing as ever. We state them in different ways to appeal to different audiences at different times, but all provide a basis for persuading people to stand behind abortion rights, both for themselves and for others.

However persuasive we are, of course, a groundswell to defend the right to abortion may not rise up until enough people feel so personally threatened that they take action. Nevertheless, if we are clear, straightforward and unabashed about why we advocate for reproductive freedom, and realistic about the threats we face, we may rebuild public support, even if this support does not instantly translate into activism. Maintaining and reinforcing this support can, in turn, ready the public for a call to action. Thus, we preserve the best hope not only for mobilizing in a crisis, but also for targeted organizing against the disparate restrictions that are building into a barrier too high for many to cross.

> "Women who have abortions are not
> impulsive monsters but people faced
> with wrenching decisions."

The Moral Complexity
of Abortion Necessitates
the Right to Choose

Jodi Enda

*Journalist Jodi Enda has covered the White House, presidential
politics, and Congress for Knight Ridder Newspapers, and was a
national correspondent for the* Philadelphia Inquirer.

*In the following selection, Enda describes how the pro-choice
movement has been put on the defensive by the aggressive media
tactics of pro-life activists. She urges women's-rights supporters
to remind the public of the continued importance of legal abortion and emphasizes the enormous effects the decision to terminate a pregnancy can have on all aspects of a woman's life.*

Kimberly was at home with her two sleeping children when
her estranged husband, high on methamphetamines and
angry about their impending divorce, showed up at her door
last September.

"He came in and said he wanted to talk about child-
support payments. We were fighting about everything. The divorce was not final," Kimberly said. "He raped me."

Kimberly didn't call the police because she wanted to protect her children from further trauma. Their lives had been

upended during the previous two and a half years, ever since she was pregnant with her younger son and discovered that her husband was an addict. Since then, he'd quit his job, and she'd worked two; he put $50,000 on their credit cards at casinos and strip clubs; he threatened to kill her when she moved out with the boys; and he stole $700 from her boss, costing her a part-time bookkeeping job. After taking medical leave because she feared a nervous breakdown, Kimberly was fired from her primary job in the business department of a Phoenix TV station.

Didn't Tell Anyone

Kimberly, then 33, didn't tell anyone about the rape, not even her closest friends. "I had no strength," she explained. Two weeks later, she realized she was pregnant. She didn't tell anyone about that, either.

She wanted an abortion, but she couldn't afford one. "I didn't know what to do," she said. "There was no way I could have had that baby. My ex would have killed me. That was never an option." Adoption wasn't, either. Kimberly couldn't bring herself to let her pregnancy show in Phoenix, and she couldn't leave town for several months the way women used to when they got pregnant out of wedlock. "I couldn't take my kids, and I couldn't leave them with my ex. I couldn't bring another child into this world. It came out of this . . . ," she said, swallowing the word "rape" as she uttered it.

So, Kimberly thought, she'd wait until she could scrape together enough money for an abortion. She had no idea how difficult that would be. "I didn't realize that the price was going up and up and up each week [as] I was going further along."

Desperate for Help

Desperate and without medical care, Kimberly went to the state for help. She qualified for Medicaid, but was told it wouldn't cover her abortion. She found a Web site that showed her how to apply to nonprofit groups for money to pay for an abortion. The Minneapolis-based Hersey Abortion Assistance Fund offered her $100, not nearly enough. Determined not to let the fetus reach the point of viability (generally interpreted to be 24 weeks gestation in Arizona), after which the state prohibits most abortions, Kimberly applied to dozens of funds around the country and sold her TV. By the end of January, she'd pulled together $900, the amount one clinic had told her was enough to cover her second-trimester abortion. She made an appointment for the two-day procedure.

When she went in the first day, the sonogram showed that she was nearly 20 weeks into her pregnancy. The abortion would cost $1,000. She didn't have it. The doctor said Kimberly would have to get the money by the next morning or postpone the procedure another week, which would drive up the price again. She sat in a park and cried.

By the next morning, Kimberly had managed to get another $100 from an abortion fund, but the delay made her miss the training session for her brand-new state job. She lost the job.

Stuck in a Tragic Situation

As I listened to Kimberly pour out her story just three weeks after her abortion, I was struck not only by the tragedy of her situation, the rawness of her emotions, but by what it meant to the larger abortion debate. Here was a mother who was struggling to take care of a 5-year-old and a 2-year-old in the face of incredible psychological and financial hardships, a woman striving to make a *moral* decision for her family. She did not want an abortion. She didn't even want the sex that led to her pregnancy. But having had the latter forced on her, she felt the former was the best response.

Decades ago, supporters of abortion rights used women like Kimberly to illustrate a need and a danger. The male doctors and clergy members who were at the forefront of the modern abortion-rights movement argued that the procedure was necessary to protect women from death or injury brought on by botched, illegal abortions. Feminists asserted that women must have control over their own lives.

Difficult Access Despite *Roe*

The movement won a tremendous victory on January 22, 1973, when the Supreme Court handed down *Roe v. Wade* and legalized abortion. Since then, abortion opponents have worked methodically, state by state, to chip away at what they saw as nearly unfettered access to abortion. Now, that access is very fettered indeed. State legislatures have passed more than 400 laws limiting access to abortion in the past decade alone. According to the Alan Guttmacher Institute, a pro-choice think tank whose statistics are cited by both sides, abortion is available in only 13 percent of U.S. counties.

Nationally, President George W. Bush in 2003 signed the first federal law—since blocked by three courts in rulings the administration is appealing—that would criminalize one or more abortion procedures. And in his second term, this most anti-abortion of presidents is almost certain to appoint some justices to the Supreme Court, potentially enough to reverse or further weaken *Roe*. (Pro-choice leaders estimate that if *Roe* were overturned, 30 states would immediately outlaw abortion except in extreme circumstances.) Meanwhile, the Republican Congress is bent on passing additional legislation to restrict access to abortion or, like the Partial-Birth Abortion Ban Act of 2003, to reduce public support for it simply by making people queasy.

Antiabortion Media Campaign

Abortion opponents have engaged in a brilliant public-relations campaign designed to manipulate the emotions of a nation that overwhelmingly supports abortion rights, but with some limits. They've used issues like "partial-birth abortion," a term they made up, to play to a general uneasiness, a discomfort felt not only by abortion opponents but by some pro-choicers as well. They've made us nervous about the "unborn," and in doing so obscured the concern we used to feel for women in dire situations.

While the right has appealed to our sentiments, the left has relied on dry legal arguments, abandoning the 1960s-style speak-outs that so successfully demonstrated why women like Kimberly need choices. But today those sorts of arguments are critical: We've just moved into an era when every woman of childbearing age has always had the right to choose abortion. Young women don't remember the hangers and back alleys; they didn't live with the fear. And now, when a right they've taken for granted is in jeopardy, virtually the only people speaking out about their choice to terminate a pregnancy are those who say they regret having made it.

An Agonizing Choice to Make

Perhaps if more people heard Kimberly's story they would understand how difficult choosing abortion can be. They would see that most women who have abortions are responsible, often poor, adults, not the reckless teens that the right often claims use abortion as birth control. In fact, 61 percent of women who have abortions are mothers, 57 percent are poor, and 78 percent report a religious affiliation, according to the Guttmacher Institute. Some can afford the $400-and-up price tag, but many can't. Often they don't know where to turn for help. Many have to travel out of town to find a clinic, to spend a night or more in hotels or cars, to miss work, to parcel out their kids. Many agonize between their own lives and children and that of a potential baby that they never intended to create.

"I felt guilty," Kimberly said, more so as the fetus grew and she felt familiar tummy flutters. "I felt I was going to be killing a baby. And there *was* a baby. . . . I had two kids. I knew what I was feeling.... It was a matter of choosing my children or this person. My children's lives would have been turned upside down. We might not be safe; we would have been worse off financially. They were already there. I had to take care of them.... *I just had to choose.*"

History of Abortion Laws

When this nation was founded, abortion was legal before "quickening," the first movement of the fetus, usually detected around four months gestation. It wasn't until the mid- to late 19th century—because of doctors' concerns for their own profession and for the safety of women, not for the well-being of fetuses—that abortion was outlawed one state at a time. "Women did terminate pregnancies in unsafe conditions, done often by nonprofessionally trained practitioners," said Kate Michelman, former president of NARAL Pro-Choice America. "The medical profession, under the aegis of wanting to protect women's health, started to campaign to make abortion illegal."

Outlawing abortion didn't end it. An estimated 700,000 to 800,000 women underwent illegal abortions each year in the 1950s and '60s. After untold numbers of women died or were maimed through the process, doctors and clergymen, mostly, who had seen the awful effects of bungled abortions in the mid-1900s, sought to reverse those laws. "It wasn't framed in terms of women's rights. It was the horrors that women were faced with," said Laura Kaplan, who wrote a book about the underground abortion movement she worked for in the early '70s in Chicago....

Antiabortion Crusade

After New York legalized abortion in 1970, and again after the Supreme Court handed down *Roe* three years later, the antiabortion movement, initially led by the Catholic hierarchy, stepped up its crusade. It took its battle to clinics—and to pregnant women themselves. Kim Gandy, president of the National Organization for Women (NOW), recalls how protesters in New Orleans, where she was living, offered juice and donuts to women seeking abortions. A nice gesture? Not exactly, Gandy said. "Our opponents knew you couldn't have an abortion if you had eaten anything because of the anesthesia." Gandy remembers her mother calling from Bossier City, Louisiana, to tell her that people were photographing women entering an abortion clinic. "From free orange juice and donuts to looking up license plates and calling up families, talking to women's husbands and kids," Gandy said. "It was bad stuff."

It would get worse. In the mid-'80s, segments of the anti-abortion movement became violent. Clinics were blockaded and firebombed, doctors who performed abortions assassinated. Although courts ruled in favor of the clinics, it was too late. Doctors were scared, and many decided to stop offering abortions.

Fight Moves to Congress

The anti-abortion forces also fought in Washington, with mixed results. In 1976, the Senate defeated the Human Life Amendment, which would have outlawed abortion. That same year, however, Congress passed the Hyde Amendment prohibiting the use of federal Medicaid money to pay for most abortions. In 1984, President Ronald Reagan enacted the so-called Mexico City policy, which blocked federal money from going to foreign organizations that perform or promote abortion overseas. In 1987, Reagan said that any program that provided abortion counseling or referrals wouldn't be eligible for money through Title X, the government's family-planning program for low-income people.

Post-*Roe* Decisions

All along, state lawmakers were passing bills to make it more difficult for women to obtain abortions. Several of the measures ended up before the Supreme Court. And while the

Court stood by the basic tenets of *Roe* it handed down two rulings in particular that effectively curbed access to abortion. In *Webster v. Reproductive Health Services*, the Court in 1989 upheld portions of a Missouri law that barred abortions in public facilities, such as hospitals, declared that life begins at conception, and required doctors to perform viability tests on fetuses after 20 weeks' gestation. Three years later, in *Planned Parenthood of Southeastern Pennsylvania v. Casey*, the Court allowed states to place restrictions on abortion prior to fetal viability as long as they didn't constitute an "undue burden" on women.

Since then, pro-choice groups have been on the defensive, trying desperately to hold back a tidal wave of anti-abortion activity in statehouses and in an increasingly conservative Congress. But the emotion that marked the abortion-rights movement's early days, the passion that spoke to people where they live, is by and large gone. It now is the province of the other side.

Abortion's Emotional Aftermath

Georgette Forney speaks frequently, publicly, and emotionally about her abortion on October 4, 1976: "I was 16 years old and living in Detroit. I didn't want my parents or anybody else to know I was sexually active. I had a good-girl image. I thought I was big enough to take care of the problem myself. And I did. . . . I remember driving to the clinic thinking, "This feels really wrong, but because it's legal, it must be OK."" During the procedure, Forney recalled, she felt violated. The stirrups bothered her. So did the "vacuum cleaner." But she moved on. "I decided to pretend it didn't happen," she said. "I did that for 19 years."

A decade ago, about five years after her daughter was born, Forney said she was flipping through her high-school yearbook when she felt a jolt. "I had this sensation that my baby was in my arms. . . . I had never allowed myself to think about what I had aborted. There I was, all of a sudden really facing what I had lost, and I was unprepared for that." She sobbed to a friend that she'd killed her baby.

Silent No More

Forney started talking openly about her experience. She founded an organization, the Silent No More Awareness Campaign, to help women like herself find ways to relieve their pain and gain forgiveness. (She's also executive director of the National Organization of Episcopalians for Life, which, along with Priests for Life, formed Silent No More.) As we talked and Forney repeated her story—for the umpteeth? hundreth? thousandth? time—she cried. In the past two years, she said, the Silent No More campaign had signed up more than 3,000 women to provide testimony at public gatherings and in TV commercials. "We don't want other people to make the same mistakes we did," Forney said. "The mistake is not just the abortion; it's assuming the abortion will solve the problem. You think you're going to walk out of the clinic and be relieved and done. You're not prepared for when you go to bed that night and hear babies crying."

Abortion Foes Employ Images

Babies crying. Unborn children. The opposition has done a lot to humanize fetuses. The emotional appeal against abortion reached its pinnacle in the last 10 years, when anti-abortion forces served up a genius campaign against what they dubbed "partial-birth abortion," a graphic term that doesn't exist in medical textbooks. Pro-choice leaders, ill-prepared to wrangle in human, as opposed to legal, terms, appeared to be twiddling their thumbs. Though not one abortion has been blocked by the ban, the gruesome images that accompanied the debate in Congress convinced even many abortion-rights supporters that this thing called "partial birth" was wrong.

Technology, too, has lent a hand to those who would end abortions. New 3D and 4D sonograms show in vivid detail what fetuses look like. How, some ask, can you abort a fetus after you've watched it suck its thumb?

Most recently, abortion battlers have proposed the Unborn Child Pain Awareness Act, which would require that providers inform women that fetuses can feel pain after 20 weeks gestation, and to offer them fetal anesthesia. (Tellingly, they don't offer money so that poor women could afford to spare their fetuses this trauma.) Pro-choice groups have been left standing on the side again.

Turning Feminism Around

Now, anti-abortion leaders are ratcheting up their emotional campaign further. Having raised sympathy for fetuses, they recently reached into the feminists' quiver to talk about what's best for women. Serrin Foster, president of Feminists for Life, contends that society has failed women by forcing them to choose between school or work and children. "We believe," she told me, "that abortion is a reflection that we have not met the needs of women."

Many Restrictions Remain

Abortion opponents haven't won yet—*Roe* is still in place—but they can take solace in numbers. Abortion rates have fallen, in part because of better birth control, but also because of state laws. "*Roe* at this point has been so eviscerated that in many respects, although I don't want to see it overturned—heavens, no—the fact is that this current Supreme Court has thus far found almost no burden undue," said Gloria Feldt, who recently resigned as president of the Planned Parenthood Federation of America.

According to NARAL, states enacted 409 anti-abortion laws in the past decade, 29 last year. NARAL reports that 47 states plus the District of Columbia allow individuals or institutions to refuse to provide women with abortions or other reproductive health services and referrals; 44 states require young women to notify or obtain consent from a parent before having an abortion though 10 of the laws have been ruled unconstitutional; 33 states plus the District of Columbia ban public financing of abortions; 30 states have mandatory waiting periods of up to three days or requirements that abortion providers give women seeking abortions negative literature or lectures; 26 states restrict the performance of abortions to hospitals or specialized facilities; and 17 states prohibit insurance from covering abortions or require women to pay higher premiums for abortion care.

Now's Gandy said that even pro-choice lawmakers mistakenly fall victim to arguments that restrictions don't hurt women. "Unfortunately, the legislators on our side don't get it," she told me. "They vote for these, what they call 'little restrictions,' all the time. It seems little to them, but the cumulative effect, or the effect on individual groups of women, can be enormous."

Abortion Providers Dwindling

As a result of restrictive laws, violence, and the stigma that has become attached to abortion, fewer doctors and other healthcare professionals are providing them. The number of abortion providers declined from a high of 2,908 in 1982 to 1,819 in 2000, a 37-percent drop, according to the Guttmacher Institute. Almost no nonmetropolitan area had an abortion provider in 2000, the institute reported, which might explain why the abortion rate among women in small towns and' rural areas is half that of women in metropolitan areas.

State restrictions almost certainly have caused some women, perhaps thousands a year, to forgo abortions. Research suggests, that Wisconsin's two-day waiting period might have contributed to a 21-percent decline in abortions there. Shawn Towey, spokeswoman for the National Network of Abortion Funds, a group comprising 102 organizations that provides money and support for low-income women seeking abortions, estimates that 60,000 women a year find the restrictions so onerous that they carry their babies to term. The Guttmacher Institute stated in a 2001 report that between 18 percent and 35 percent of Medicaid-eligible women who want to have abortions continue their pregnancies if public funding isn't available.

Low-Income Women Most Affected

"The biggest chunk of women who are unable to get abortions right now are poor women on Medicaid," said Towey. While 17 states do pay for the abortions of low-income women, 33 do not. "The big irony," she said, "is that low-income women get later abortions because they have to delay to save the money." The Guttmacher report said that 22 percent Medicaid-eligible women who had second-trimester abortions would have ended their pregnancies earlier if the government paid.

And behind every one of these numbers lies the story of a woman.

Rights Movement "in a Bind"

The good news, if there is any, is that women's rights activists are waking up to their public-relations problem. "I think we have to face the reality that public support for abortion is eroding," said Martha Burk, chair of the National Council of Women's Organizations. "I think we've clearly lost the terminology war. They keep coming up with very reasonable-sounding restrictions, and we are unable to counter that. . . . The movement is in a bind."

Feldt said, "For way too many years, the pro-choice movement was reacting to things. They thought they had won, and when you win you only have to defend. When you are in a defensive posture, your adversaries will nibble off one finger at a time, and pretty soon your whole arm is gone." That's precisely what happened when Congress passed the 2003 abortion ban, Feldt said.

"The ban . . . was not our finest moment," Michelman agreed. "We got caught up on numbers and procedures and we allowed the other side to define the terrain."

Neither were pro-choice leaders helped by the 2004 Democratic nominee for president, John Kerry, who said that he personally opposed abortion but supported a woman's right to choose. "He seemed equivocal. He ceded the moral high ground to the other side," Feldt told The Associated Press after resigning from Planned Parenthood in January.

Common Ground or Clever Tactics

The solution du jour is a clever tactic to trap the anti-abortion side in a seeming contradiction. Join us, pro-choice leaders are saying, in reducing the need for abortions. "The fact is that the best way to reduce the number of abortions is to reduce the number of unwanted pregnancies in the first place," Hillary Rodham Clinton told abortion-rights supporters in January [2005] as she pressed to find "common ground" with opponents. In February, NARAL placed an ad in the conservative *Weekly Standard* asking abortion opponents to "Please, help us prevent abortions." The ad encouraged abortion foes to support a bill introduced by Senate Minority Leader Harry Reid, a Democrat who opposes abortion, that aims to reduce unintended pregnancies by making contraceptives and family-planning services more readily available. The Prevention First Act would require insurance policies that pay for prescription medications to cover birth control, promote emergency contraception (particularly for rape victims), and improve sex education.

The NARAL challenge represents a cunning strategy, if only because it allows pro-choice advocates to define the terms of the debate. "They have avoided wanting to talk about prevention," said the group's new president, Nancy Keenan. "Instead of us always discussing issues that they want to talk about, let's talk about the issues that we want to talk about."

Opponents Not Taking the Bait

Anti-abortion groups are unlikely to engage in the discussion. They haven't so far, and most of them either reject or simply ignore the question of birth control. Even Feminists for Life doesn't take a position on contraception. (Eleanor Smeal, president of the Feminist Majority Foundation, told me that she tried to compromise with abortion opponents while head of NOW in the 1980s. But, she said, "There is no common ground on increasing family planning. They're opposed to family planning.")

That might not matter now. This isn't a campaign to win over anti-abortion leaders. It's a campaign like the other side's "partial-birth" strategy—to appeal to middle Americans, the vast majority of whom use contraception and support abortion rights to some degree. As Clinton acknowledged in her speech, the search for common ground needs to go hand in hand with a campaign to demonstrate that women who have abortions are not impulsive monsters but people faced with wrenching decisions. "I believe we can all recognize that abortion in many ways represents a sad, even tragic choice to many, many women," Clinton said. "This decision is a profound and complicated one; a difficult one, often the most difficult that a woman will ever make."

Issue Essential to Women's Lives

The choice itself—the opportunity to decide—is essential to women's lives. Burk put it like this: "It's not just about whether and when to have children. It's about timing. It's about being able to be free of abusive relationships . . . the ability to go ahead with a career. . . . It's about how your life unfolds. It can mean the difference in being dependent on government largesse or not for great periods of your life. It can mean the difference in the quality of life for your other children." It can mean, she said, not having a baby at the age of 12. It can mean surviving.

But when politicians and lobbyists argue, it's rarely about 12-year-old girls. More likely, it's about 12-week-old fetuses.

It's time to turn the conversation back—back to women, back to children, back to people who have been born. Frances Kissling, president of Catholics for a Free Choice, said this might mean acknowledging the growing connection Americans have to fetuses, and the moral complexity behind abortion. Pro-choice leaders need to talk about abortion the way women talk about it at their kitchen tables, Kissling asserted. "My experience with women at abortion clinics is they largely understand the nuances of what's going on," she said. "They do not come in waving the flag and pounding their shoe on the table demanding an abortion as a political right. They come in . . . as rich human beings dealing with a conflict of values. They come in fully aware that the life that is developing within them has value. To me that doesn't give it rights, that doesn't make it a person. Its developing humanity still comes into conflict with women's lives and aspirations."

It's that sense of the fetus that's convinced some in the pro-choice movement that they should stand back during the upcoming congressional debate on the "fetal pain" bill, which wouldn't restrict abortion, but which would continue to humanize fetuses.

A Need to Balance Sympathies

The challenge for pro-choicers is to balance America's growing sympathy for fetuses with an equal—or greater—concern for women. They must counter the image of a humanized fetus with that of a human, caring, and sometimes suffering woman—with a woman who has needs and feelings and morals. The argument won't win over staunch abortion foes. But it should strike a chord with mainstream Americans, the very people the abortion-rights movement needs to reach. The pro-choice movement must speak the language of real people—and maybe even let real people, like Kimberly, speak.

"The Court has never held that what is a protected constitutional right today would not be a protected constitutional right tomorrow."

The Supreme Court Will Not Overrule Abortion Laws

Robert A. Sedler

Robert A. Sedler is a law professor and lawyer who litigated the Kentucky version of Roe v. Wade *for the American Civil Liberties Union of Kentucky.*

In the following essay, Sedler contends that the U.S. Supreme Court will not reverse Roe v. Wade, *noting that historically the Court has refused to withdraw basic constitutional rights established in prior cases regardless of the apparent political leanings of individual justices. Sedler refutes the theory that the appointment of conservative judges to the Court since* Roe v. Wade *was decided in 1973 might result in the case being overturned. Sedler further remarks that the court is unlikely to tamper with a decision that has become ingrained in American society and involves such a personal, individual decision.*

The recent confirmation of two purportedly conservative Justices to the Supreme Court has fueled media speculation that the Supreme Court may be "poised to overrule *Roe v. Wade.*" The speculation has been fanned by South Dakota's recent enactment of a law banning virtually all abortions for

Robert A. Sedler, "The Supreme Court Will Not Overrule *Roe v. Wade*," *Hofstra Law Review*, vol. 34, Spring 2006, pp. 1207–13. © 2006 Hofstra University. All rights reserved. Reproduced by permission.

the stated purpose of getting the Supreme Court to reconsider *Roe*. The pro-life forces also take encouragement from the fact that the Court has agreed to hear the government's appeal from lower court decisions holding unconstitutional Congress's ban on "partial birth" abortions. Finally, based on the assumption by the pro-life forces that there are now four Justices on the Court willing to overrule *Roe* (Chief Justice Roberts, and Justices Scalia, Thomas and Alito), the possible retirement of Justice Stevens and his replacement by a Bush-appointed "pro-life" Justice would ensure the overruling of *Roe*, and with it a woman's constitutional right to make the choice to end an unwanted pregnancy by a safe and legal abortion.

The problem with this scenario is that it is completely wrong. The Supreme Court will not overrule *Roe v. Wade*. This is so for two related reasons, one going to the operation of the Court itself, and the other going to the value acceptances of American society today.

The Court operates as an institution, and the new Justices, like the other Justices on the Court, will operate within this institutional framework. We can understand the workings of the Court as an institution by looking to what it has done over a number of years, and we can assume that what it has done in the past, it will continue to do in the future.

Constitutional Doctrine and Precedent

The most important component in Supreme Court decision-making is the constitutional doctrine and precedent that has emerged from the Court's decisions in the different areas of constitutional law over a period of time. Most of the constitutional cases coming before the Court today, important as some of them may be in terms of public policy and societal impact, involve the application of this doctrine and precedent to particular constitutional questions, some very narrow, arising from new laws and new kinds of governmental action. While media commentary (and sometimes academic commentary as well) might suggest that the Court, particularly as its composition changes, frequently reviews its major and most controversial decisions, experience indicates that this indeed is not the case. Although the Court has the power to overrule its prior decisions and sometimes does so, a longitudinal analysis indicates that over a period of time comparatively few decisions have been overruled. Generally, the court will overrule a decision only when its premises have been weakened by subsequent decisions, so that there is a seeming inconsistency between the older and newer decisions, or when the Court concludes in retrospect that the decision could not be supported by the doctrine and precedents on which it was based. The Court has never overruled a decision, at least not explicitly, on the ground that the composition of the Court has changed, and a majority of the present Justices would have decided the case differently had they been on the Court at the time of the decision.

The Court Guards Basic Interests

More importantly for present purposes, the Court has never overruled a decision recognizing a constitutional liberty interest or for that matter any other constitutionally-protected interest. The Court has never held that what is a protected constitutional right today would not be a protected constitutional right tomorrow. Where the Court has overruled cases involving constitutional rights, it has been to overrule a case rejecting a claimed constitutional right and to hold that the claimed right is indeed protected by the Constitution.

Roe v. Wade was a landmark decision, holding that a woman has a protected liberty interest in making the choice to have a safe and legal abortion. That decision has been the law of the land for some thirty-three years. And in the 1992 case of *Planned Parenthood of Southeastern Pennsylvania v. Casey*, the Court expressly affirmed the central holding of *Roe v. Wade*, that a woman had a fundamental right to make the choice to have an abortion prior to the time that the fetus became viable while permitting only such regulation of the abortion procedure that it did not impose an "undue burden" on the woman's right to choose to have an abortion.

Principles of *Roe* Have Not Changed

In *Casey*, the Court specifically rejected the argument of the pro-life forces, joined in by the first Bush administration, and supported by four dissenting Justices, that it should overrule *Roe v. Wade*. The Court noted that there were no grounds for overruling *Roe* in terms of its premises having been weakened by subsequent decisions or its being unsupported by the doctrine and premises on which it was based. Indeed, the only thing that had changed was the composition of the Court, and this had never been considered to be a proper ground for overruling a prior decision.

More importantly, in *Casey* the Court explained why it had never overruled a precedent recognizing a constitutional liberty interest. As Justice Kennedy succinctly put it: "In *Casey* we noted that when a court is asked to overrule a precedent recognizing a constitutional liberty interest, individual or societal reliance on the existence of that liberty cautions with particular strength against reversing course." As the Court stated in *Casey*:

> Abortion is customarily chosen as an unplanned response to the consequence of unplanned activity or to the failure of conventional birth control, and except on the assumption that no intercourse would have occurred but for *Roe's* holding, such behavior may appear to justify no reliance claim. . . .

> To eliminate the issue of reliance that easily, however, one would need to limit cognizable reliance to specific instances of sexual activity. But to do this would be simply to refuse to face the fact that for two decades of economic and social developments, people have organized intimate relationships

and made choices that define their views of themselves and their places in society, *in reliance on the availability of abortion in the event that contraception should fail.* The ability of women to participate equally in the economic and social life of the Nation has been facilitated by their ability to control their reproductive lives. The Constitution serves human values, and while the effect of reliance on *Roe* cannot be exactly measured, neither can the certain cost of overruling *Roe* for people who have ordered their thinking and living around that case be dismissed.

Fourteen more years have elapsed since *Casey* decided, and the reasons set forth by the Court in *Casey* that "caution with particular strength against reversing course" apply even more strongly today. The Supreme Court operates as an institution, and for the Court to overrule *Roe v. Wade* today would be completely inconsistent with the Court's institutional behavior over a long period of time.

Overruling *Roe* Would Disrupt Society

The second and related reason why the Court will not overrule *Roe v. Wade* today is that this would have a cataclysmic effect on American society. For large numbers of American women, abortion has become a fully acceptable way of ending an unwanted pregnancy. Approximately 1.3 million abortions are performed in the United States each year. Almost 90% of the abortions are performed during the first twelve weeks, with most being performed during the first nine weeks. Less than 1% of these abortions are performed after twenty-four weeks. In 2002, the last year for which figures are available, 60% of the women having abortions were already mothers, which shows that for these women at least, abortion was a "back-up" for contraception. And, emphasizing the importance of choice, the figures also show that 53% of the women having unwanted pregnancies chose to continue with their pregnancies rather than have an abortion.

There is thus a disconnect between the media speculation that the Supreme Court may be "poised to overrule *Roe v. Wade*" and the real world in which American women live their lives. Women under fifty came of age at a time when women had the right to choose to end an unwanted pregnancy by a safe and legal abortion. Every day in America some women faced with an unwanted pregnancy choose to have an abortion while a like number of women choose to continue their pregnancy. *A woman's right to choose is a part of the value acceptances of American society today.* I strongly suspect that a clear majority of Americans would support a woman's right to choose to have an abortion during the first nine to twelve weeks of pregnancy, which is when most abortions take place. Less than 1% of abortions are performed after twenty-four weeks, presumably to protect the life or health of the woman. I would assume that many of the abortions performed between ten and twenty-four weeks are because ultrasound or genetic testing has revealed that the woman is carrying a seriously defective fetus, and here too I strongly suspect that a clear majority of Americans would support the woman's right to choose in this very difficult situation. In other words, when it comes to the crucial issue of the women's right to choose to have an abortion in the circumstances where in fact American woman do chose to have an abortion—as opposed to peripheral issues such as parental consent or notification or a ban on so-called "partial birth abortion"—I maintain that a clear majority of Americans would support a woman's right to choose to end a pregnancy by a safe and legal abortion. It is my submission then, that a woman's right to choose is a part of the value acceptances of American society today.

The Supreme Court is not going to take that choice away from American women, no matter who joins its ranks. The Supreme Court is not going to overrule *Roe v. Wade*.

> *"One suspects there will be no Damascus road conversion over abortion for Alito, and that the reversal of* Roe *will raise a storm not seen since* Brown *overturned segregation."*

A Conservative Supreme Court Could Overturn Abortion Laws

Nicholas Hill and Peter Ling

Nicholas Hill is training to be a lawyer and Peter Ling is a professor of American studies at the University of Nottingham, England.

In the following article, published in England, Hill and Ling review past decisions by conservative justices of the U.S. Supreme Court, particularly those in cases that involve racial discrimination. The authors explore how the reasoning in these rulings has led some to predict that the Court will overturn its 1973 decision in Roe v. Wade.

W ith the Christian Right's growing political influence, abortion divides Americans like few other issues. The Supreme Court is due shortly to rule on two cases, one from California, the other from Nebraska, and both claim that the actions of US Attorney General Gonzales under the 2003 Partial-Birth Abortion Ban Act are unconstitutional as they deny the right to abortion granted under *Roe v. Wade* (1973).

Nicholas Hill and Peter Ling, "Brewing Up a Storm," *History Today*, vol. 56, October 2006, pp. 38–39. Reproduced by permission.

For conservatives, legal protection of abortion epitomizes the toxic legacy of 1960s' social policy. It is contrary to the ideal of deliberately limited government in American life as well as to religious principles. For liberals, Roe is part of the rights revolution, an extension of federal protection and of guaranteed equality, and thus reflects the same philosophy that underpinned the desegregation policy launched by the Supreme Court's *Brown v. Board of Education* (1954) decision.

Justices Politically Insulated

As final interpreters of the Constitution, the Court's nine Justices will rule on the matter. Unelected, serving for life, and insulated from executive pressure and public backlash, their power to impose their own principles is potentially more sweeping and less accountable than any other branch of government. Each Justice is nominated by the President and confirmed by Senate vote after judiciary committee hearings. This process should reveal a nominee's true character, but senators can miss storm signals, as they did in the case of William Hubbs Rehnquist, who served on the Court for thirty-three years, fourteen of them as Associate Justice (1972–86), nineteen as Chief Justice to (2005).

In 1971 the law backed desegregation as a means of ensuring racial equality through government action. The policy grew principally from the Supreme Court's *Brown v. Board of Education* decision that racially separate educational facilities were inherently unequal. This reversed the Court's position, first outlined in *Plessy v. Ferguson* (1896), that 'separate but equal facilities' were permissible. The Court's order for school districts to desegregate with 'all deliberate speed' was resisted vigorously, and further rulings were needed to implement it. In the less well-known but more important case of *Green v. County School Board* (1968) the Court declared that local education authorities had an 'affirmative duty' to ensure racial discrimination was 'eliminated root and branch'. Two years

later, *Swann v. Charlotte-Mecklenburg Board of Education*
(1971) allowed federal courts to use broad measures to ensure
integration or racial balance—including the controversial practice of bussing children to different schools.

Rehnquist Steps In

Despite turbulence across the country over the nature of integration as a principle, and bussing as a practice, no Justice
wrote a dissent over desegregation for nearly two decades after
Brown. That calm ended when Rehnquist became an Associate
Justice in 1972. Proposed by President Nixon, Rehnquist came
before a nominally Democratic Senate that had tilted towards
conservatism in the 1970 mid-term elections. Nevertheless, the
Senate could have rejected him as they had rejected a previous
Nixon nominee, Harold Carswell. Realizing that he was seen
as being more to the right than Nixon, Rehnquist was studi-
ously noncommittal at his 1971 confirmation hearings, but
was pinned down on school desegregation. The hearings scrutinized Rehnquist's letter to his local Arizona newspaper in
1970 in which he had denounced desegregation proposals,
complaining that 'Those who would abandon [the existing
neighborhood school system] concern themselves not with the
great majority . . . but with a small minority.' By small minority, Rehnquist meant, of course, Phoenix's African-American
population. Quizzed by senators, Rehnquist admitted that his
opinion was unchanged. While he appeared to accept the ending of *de jure* (legally imposed) segregation as required by
Brown, he was evasive over *de facto* segregation (as a by-
product of residential segregation). He couldn't answer, he
claimed, because the matter was currently before the Court
and he might well be bound by that precedent.

In the early 1950s Rehnquist had served as law clerk for
Justice Robert Jackson. The discovery of a memo Rehnquist
had written as Jackson's clerk during the *Brown* case should
have ended any doubt about his views. It included the decla-

ration 'I think *Plessy v. Ferguson* was right and should be reaffirmed.' In other words, legal precedent protected segregation. When challenged, an unnerved Rehnquist tried to deny that he preferred the 'separate but equal' principle of *Plessy* by implying that these were the private views of Justice Jackson. Yet despite evasiveness on a crucial constitutional question, Rehnquist was confirmed by sixty-eight votes to twenty-six.

Views Become Clear

His true views were soon evident. In *Keyes v. School District No. 1* (1973), he argued that *de jure* and *de facto* segregation were not the same 'constitutional violation'. By an illegitimate stretching of logic from the *Brown* case, he fumed, the Court had proceeded without constitutional justification in *Green* to demand that school boards 'affirmatively undertake to achieve racial mixing in schools' in cases where what Rehnquist disingenuously called 'neutrally drawn boundary lines' did not produce the requisite mix. Soon, his many dissents, including one in *Roe v. Wade* earned him a nickname: 'The Lone Ranger'.

No Longer Alone

By 1986, when he became Chief Justice, Rehnquist was no longer alone. Successful nominations to the Supreme Court by Ronald Reagan and George Bush Sr. had made him part of a 5-1 conservative majority. *In Board of Education of Oklahoma City v. Dowell* (1991) his opinion overturned the substance of the *Green* decision and reversed the Court's direction since *Brown*. Rehnquist condemned a lower court ruling that the Oklahoma City school board had not met its affirmative duty to eliminate segregation as 'draconian' and as imposing an unconstitutional burden since it had 'done nothing for 25 years to promote residential segregation', which was 'the result of private decision making' for which the school board could not be held responsible. A year later in *Freeman v. Pitts* the Court essentially gave its blessing to *de facto* segregation by declaring that 'where resegregation is a product and not of state action but of private choices, it does not have constitutional implications'. By 1995 the Rehnquist Court was more likely to condemn than to applaud desegregation efforts. While a theoretical commitment to racial equality in *Brown* remained, its practical application was no longer sought.

Alito Shows Parallels

The most recent addition to the Supreme Court, Samuel Alito, offers striking parallels. At the time of his nomination in 2005, it was widely reported that Alito, a constitutional lawyer, was openly hostile to the liberal interventionist jurisprudence. Just as Rehnquist's early writings warned of his dogmatic goals, documents relating to Alito's time as a lawyer in Ronald Reagan's Justice Department expose a similar sense of conservative mission, this time over abortion.

In a 1985 job application, Alito wrote 'I am particularly proud of my contribution in recent cases in which the government has argued in the Supreme Court that ... the Constitution does not protect a right to an abortion. In *Roe v. Wade*, the Court had established this right and struck down all state abortion laws. As an assistant to the Solicitor General, Alito wrote a memo in 1985 on the case of *Thornburgh v. American College of Obstetricians and Gynecologists* which, he argued, gave the Reagan administration a great chance to challenge the current constitutional position. The White House should 'make clear that we disagree with *Roe v. Wade*' and should not 'even tacitly concede *Roe's* legitimacy'.

Eroding *Roe's* Precedent

Alito's later circuit court rulings confirm his desire to reverse the *Roe* precedent. In *Planned Parenthood of Southeastern Pennsylvania v. Casey* (1991) Judge Alito affirmed a state law that made it obligatory in all cases to provide information about alternatives to abortion, to impose a waiting period of at least twenty-four hours and to require parental consent for minors. His fellow judges only demurred when Alito added that he believed a woman must notify her husband when seeking an abortion. A bitterly divided Supreme Court struck down this part of the ruling in 1992 because it constituted an 'undue burden'. But Alito's proposed requirement also directly contravened the right to privacy that unpinned the right to abortion guaranteed in 1973. When a Supreme Court ruling in 2000 rendered moot a Pennsylvania case arising from a ban on partial-birth abortion, Judge Alito felt compelled to carp at the required compliance of his court. His outspokenness underlined how federal protection of abortion rights is as anathema [loathed] to him as federal insistence on racial integration was for Rehnquist.

Although Alito faced Senate confirmation before a Republican-dominated committee, he still knew that an outspoken attack on abortion could derail his nomination. When Senator Arlen Specter raised the *Roe* and *Casey* cases, Alito responded that the presumption should be 'that the court will follow its prior precedents' [i.e. *Roe*] adding that there had to be 'a special justification for overruling a prior precedent'.

Alito Noncommittal on *Roe*

To illustrate his argument, Alito noted that even though Rehnquist had disagreed with the *Miranda v. Arizona* (1966) ruling that required police to warn criminal suspects regarding possible self—incrimination, as Chief Justice in *Dickerson v. United States* (2000) he had nevertheless followed the *Miranda* precedent. Since 1966, Rehnquist had explained, 'the *Miranda* warning had become embedded in routine police practice to a point where the warnings have become part of our national culture'. Asked whether he believed that *Roe v. Wade* had become similarly embedded, Alito was as noncommittal as Rehnquist had been on school desegregation decades earlier.

We await the Court's verdict in the pending abortion cases. When the Court last considered the matter in 2000, its ruling incensed Federal Judge Alito. On that occasion, Justice Sandra Day O'Conner provided the swing vote in a 5-4 majority verdict. Alito is now her successor. Will he bow to precedent as he implied at his confirmation hearings? Or will he, like Rehnquist on school desegregation, remain true to his own principles? One suspects there will be no Damascus road conversion [An abrupt about-face] over abortion for Alito, and that the reversal of *Roe* will raise a storm not seen since *Brown* overturned segregation.

CHAPTER 2

Gender Equity in the Workplace

Case Overview

Corning Glass Works
v. Brennan (1974)

Corning Glass Works v. Brennan was the first case to reach the U.S. Supreme Court that involved the Equal Pay Act of 1963 (EPA), a groundbreaking federal law intended to ensure "equal pay for equal work" regardless of a worker's gender. The Court ruled in *Corning* that an employer had violated the EPA by allowing female workers to remain at a lower pay rate than male coworkers who performed the same job.

Until World War II, women rarely worked in traditionally male-dominated jobs, including technical jobs in manufacturing plants. The notion that women were unsuited for such jobs was embedded in the culture and in laws that restricted women's right to work. Women who did work outside the home earned far less than men. World War II forced employers to hire women to take over jobs abandoned by men who had been sent overseas to fight. However, the overall pay disparity for women persisted.

Corning involved two factories operated by Corning Glass Works. For years, only women held the job of inspecting finished glass products at the plants. In 1925 the company created a nighttime inspection shift. However, only men were hired for the night jobs because state laws in place at the time prohibited women from working at night. The night-shift male inspectors, who transferred from higher-paying jobs within the plant, were paid more than the female day-shift inspectors, even though the work was identical. In 1944 Corning added a pay increase for the night-shift workers, still all male. This further increased the pay differential between the nighttime male inspectors and daytime female inspectors. In 1966, after the EPA was enacted by Congress and the laws barring women from night work had been repealed, Corning began to allow women to work at night and apply for the higher-paying night inspection jobs. In 1969 the company removed the day/night pay differential for inspectors hired after that point. However, the pay of previously hired inspectors—the lower-paid women and higher-paid men remained at the rates dictated by the old pay system.

The female inspectors sued Corning under the EPA, claiming they were not receiving equal pay despite doing equal work. Separate suits were filed for the women working in each of the two plants, which were located in different states. The federal trial court and court of appeals in one case reached a differing conclusion from the trial and appeals courts in the other case. The Supreme Court accepted the case to resolve the differing outcomes. The Court ruled that Corning had violated the EPA by allowing a pay system to continue under which women were paid less than men for the same job duties. The Court held that Corning's efforts to correct the disparity failed, as previously hired female inspectors continued to be paid less than their male counterparts.

When the EPA was enacted, U.S. women earned approximately 59 percent of men's wages on average. *Corning* and subsequent litigation, combined with other equal-pay laws, gradually narrowed the pay gap over the following four decades. However, women's pay still averages less than 80 percent of men's. The major reason the EPA has not done more to reduce the male-female wage gap is that the statute applies only in situations where men and women work for the same employer doing similar jobs. The law does not address the fact that many women continue to work in so-called "pink-collar" jobs, such as clerical work, healthcare assistance, housekeeping, and childcare. Overall, these jobs pay less than commonly male-dominated occupations such as construction work, engineering, and business management. Those seeking to eliminate the persisting wage gap support such measures as stronger enforcement of the EPA, greater use of additional anti-discrimination laws, and union representation of more female workers.

"*The whole purpose of the Act was to require that these depressed wages be raised, in part as a matter of simple justice to the employees themselves, but also as a matter of market economics, since Congress recognized as well that discrimination in wages on the basis of sex 'constitutes an unfair method of competition.'*"

The Court's Decision: The Equal Pay Act Prohibits a Wage Differential between Men and Women for Equal Work Under Similar Working Conditions

Justice Thurgood Marshall

Justice Thurgood Marshall was born in 1908 in Baltimore, Maryland. In 1933 he graduated from Howard University Law School in Washington, D.C. For over twenty years, Justice Marshall fought racial segregation through his legal work with the NAACP (National Association for the Advancement of Colored People). He argued the U.S. Supreme Court case of Brown v. Board of Education *in 1954, and was assigned to the United States Court of Appeals for the Second Circuit in 1961. Justice Marshall was appointed to the U.S. Supreme Court by President Lyndon B. Johnson in 1967. He served on the Court until 1991 and died two years later at the age of eighty-four.*

Justice Thurgood Marshall, majority opinion, *Corning Glass Works v. Brennan*, 417 U.S. 188, 1974.

Corning Glass Works v. Brennan *was a key case in the battle by women to receive equal pay for doing the same work as their male counterparts. The case was decided by the U.S. Supreme Court in 1974. The following article is an excerpt from the majority opinion in the case written by Justice Marshall. The Court ruled that Corning Glass Works had violated the Equal Pay Act of 1963 by paying its night-shift inspectors, all of whom were male, more than females who performed the same work during the day. The Court further found that Corning's later decision to allow women to work the night shift did not solve the pay disparity because female day inspectors were still paid less than night inspectors. The Court also held that an additional effort by Corning, which equalized day and night inspector wage rates, did not end the discrimination because the new rates applied only to newly hired employees and were not retroactive for existing workers.*

Congress' purpose in enacting the Equal Pay Act was to remedy what was perceived to be a serious and endemic problem of employment discrimination in private industry—the fact that the wage structure of "many segments of American industry has been based on an ancient but outmoded belief that a man, because of his role in society, should be paid more than a woman even though his duties are the same." The solution adopted was quite simple in principle: to require that "equal work will be rewarded by equal wages."

The Act's basic structure and operation are similarly straightforward. In order to make out a case under the Act, the [U.S. secretary of labor] must show that an employer pays different wages to employees of opposite sexes "for equal work on jobs the performance of which requires equal skill, effort, and responsibility, and which are performed under similar working conditions." Although the Act is silent on this point, its legislative history makes plain that the Secretary has the burden of proof on this issue, as both of the courts below recognized. [Case citations omitted throughout.]

Exceptions to Equal Pay Rule

The Act also establishes four exceptions—three specific and one a general catchall provision—where different payment to employees of opposite sexes "is made pursuant to (i) a seniority system; (ii) a merit system; (iii) a system which measures earnings by quantity or quality of production; or (iv) a differential based on any other factor other than sex." Again, while the Act is silent on this question, its structure and history also suggest that once the Secretary has carried his burden of showing that the employer pays workers of one sex more than workers of the opposite sex for equal work, the burden shifts to the employer to show that the differential is justified under one of the Act's four exceptions. All of the many lower courts that have considered this question have so held, and this view is consistent with the general rule that the application or an exemption under the Fair Labor Standards Act is a matter of affirmative defense on which the employer has the burden of proof.

The contentions of the parties in this case reflect the Act's underlying framework. Corning argues that the Secretary has failed to prove that Corning ever violated the Act because day shift work is not "performed under similar working conditions" as night shift work. The Secretary maintains that day shift and night shift work are performed under "similar working conditions" within the meaning of the Act. Although the Secretary recognizes that higher wages may be paid for night shift work, the Secretary contends that such a shift differential would be based upon a "factor other than sex" within the catchall exception to the Act and that Corning has failed to carry its burden of proof that its higher base wage for male night inspectors was in fact based on any factor other than sex.

Conflicting Statements by Congress

The courts below relied in part on conflicting statements in the legislative history having some bearing on this question of statutory construction. The Third Circuit found particularly significant a statement of Congressman Goodell, a sponsor of the Equal Pay bill, who, in the course of explaining the bill on the floor of the House, commented that "standing as opposed to sitting, pleasantness or unpleasantness of surroundings, periodic rest periods, hours of work, difference in shift, all would logically fall within the working condition factor." The Second Circuit, in contrast, relied on a statement from the House Committee Report which, in describing the broad general exception for differentials "based on any other factor other than sex," stated: "Thus, among other things, shift differentials . . . would also be excluded. . . ."

We agree with Judge Friendly, however, that in this case a better understanding of the phrase "performed under similar working conditions" can be obtained from a consideration of the way in which Congress arrived at the statutory language than from trying to reconcile or establish preferences between the conflicting interpretations of the Act by individual legislators or the committee reports. As Mr. Justice Felix Frankfurter remarked in an earlier case involving interpretation of the Fair Labor Standards Act, "regard for the specific history of the legislative process that culminated in the Act now before us affords more solid ground for giving it appropriate meaning."

The most notable feature of the history of the Equal Pay Act is that Congress recognized early in the legislative process that the concept of equal pay for equal work was more readily stated in principle than reduced to statutory language which would be meaningful to employers and workable across the broad range of industries covered by the Act. As originally introduced, the Equal Pay bill required equal pay for "equal work on jobs the performance of which requires equal skills." There were only two exceptions—for differentials "made pursuant to a seniority or merit increase system which does not discriminate on the basis of sex. . . ."

Methods to Measure Job Value

In both the House and Senate committee hearings, witnesses were highly critical of the Act's definition of equal work and of its exemptions. Many noted that most of American industry used formal, systematic job evaluation plans to establish equitable wage structures in their plants. Such systems, as explained coincidentally by a representative of Corning Glass Works who testified at both hearings, took into consideration four separate factors in determining job value—skill, effort, responsibility and working conditions—and each of these four components was further systematically divided into various subcomponents. Under a job evaluation plan, point values are assigned to each of the subcomponents of a given job, resulting in a total point figure representing a relatively objective measure of the job's value.

In comparison to the rather complex job evaluation plans used by industry, the definition of equal work used in the first drafts of the Equal Pay bill was criticized as unduly vague and incomplete. Industry representatives feared that as a result of the bill's definition of equal work, the Secretary of Labor would be cast in the position of second-guessing the validity of a company's job evaluation system. They repeatedly urged that the bill be amended to include an exception for job classification systems, or otherwise to incorporate the language of job evaluation into the bill. Thus Corning's own representative testified:

> "Job evaluation is an accepted and tested method of attaining equity in wage relationship.

> "A great part of industry is committed to job evaluation by past practice and by contractual agreement as the basis for wage administration.

> "'Skill' alone, as a criterion, fails to recognize other aspects of the job situation that affect job worth.

"We sincerely hope that this committee in passing legislation to eliminate wage differences based on sex alone, will recognize in its language the general role of job evaluation in establishing equitable rate relationship."

Defining "Equal Work"

We think it plain that in amending the bill's definition of equal work to its present form, the Congress acted in direct response to these pleas. Spokesmen for the amended bill stated, for example, during the House debates:

"The concept of equal pay for jobs demanding equal skill has been expanded to require also equal effort, responsibility, and similar working conditions. These factors are the core of all job classification systems. They form a legitimate basis for differentials in pay."

Indeed, the most telling evidence of congressional intent is the fact that the Act's amended definition of equal work incorporated the specific language of the job evaluation plan described at the hearings by Corning's own representative—that is, the concepts of "skill," "effort," "responsibility," and "working conditions."

Non-Discriminating Pay Differences Acceptable

Congress' intent, as manifested in this history, was to use these terms to incorporate into the new federal Act the well-defined and well-accepted principles of job evaluation so as to ensure that wage differentials based upon bona fide job evaluation plans would be outside the purview of the Act. The House Report emphasized:

"This language recognizes that there are many factors which may be used to measure the relationships between jobs and which establish a valid basis for a difference in pay. These factors will be found in a majority of the job classification systems. Thus, it is anticipated that a bona fide job classification program that does not discriminate on the basis of sex will serve as a valid defense to a charge of discrimination."

Exploring the Meaning of "Working Conditions"

It is in this light that the phrase "working conditions" must be understood, for where Congress has used technical words or terms of art, "it [is] proper to explain them by reference to the art or science to which they [are] appropriate." This principle is particularly salutary [favorable] where, as here, the legislative history reveals that Congress incorporated words having a special meaning within the field regulated by the statute so as to overcome objections by industry representatives that statutory definitions were vague and incomplete.

While a layman might well assume that time of day worked reflects one aspect of a job's "working conditions," the term has a different and much more specific meaning in the language of industrial relations. As Corning's own representative testified at the hearings, the element of working conditions encompasses two subfactors: "surroundings" and "hazards." "Surroundings" measures the elements, such as toxic chemicals or fumes, regularly encountered by a worker, their intensity, and their frequency. "Hazards" takes into account the physical hazards regularly encountered, their frequency, and the severity of injury they can cause. This definition of "working conditions" is not only manifested in Corning's own job evaluation plans but is also well accepted across a wide range of American industry.

Night Shift Pay Policy Found Discriminatory

Nowhere in any of these definitions is time of day worked mentioned as a relevant criterion. The fact of the matter is that the concept of "working conditions," as used in the specialized language of job evaluation systems, simply does not encompass shift differentials. Indeed, while Corning now argues that night inspection work is not equal to day inspection work, all of its own job evaluation plans, including the one now in effect, have consistently treated them as equal in all respects, including working conditions. And Corning's Manager of Job Evaluation testified . . . that time of day worked was not considered to be a "working condition." Significantly, it is not the Secretary in this case who is trying to look behind Corning's bona fide job evaluation system to require equal pay for jobs which Corning has historically viewed as unequal work. Rather, it is Corning which asks us to differentiate between jobs which the company itself has always equated. We agree with the Second Circuit that the inspection work at issue in this case, whether performed during the day or night, is "equal work" as that term is defined in the Act.

This does not mean, of course, that there is no room in the Equal Pay Act for nondiscriminatory shift differentials. Work on a steady night shift no doubt has psychological and physiological impacts making it less attractive than work on a day shift. The Act contemplates that a male night worker may receive a higher wage than a female day worker, just as it contemplates that a male employee with 20 years' seniority can receive a higher wage than a woman with two years' seniority. Factors such as these play a role under the Act's four exceptions—the seniority differential under the specific seniority exception, the shift differential under the catchall exception for differentials "based on any other factor other than sex."

The question remains, however, whether Corning carried its burden of proving that the higher rate paid for night inspection work, until 1966 performed solely by men, was in fact intended to serve as compensation for night work, or rather constituted an added payment based upon sex. We agree that the record amply supports the District Court's conclusion that Corning had not sustained its burden of proof. As its history revealed, "the higher night rate was in large part the product of the generally higher wage level of male workers and the need to compensate them for performing what were regarded as demeaning tasks." The differential in base wages originated at a time when no other night employees received higher pay than corresponding day workers, and it was maintained long after the company instituted a separate plant-wide shift differential which was thought to compensate adequately for the additional burdens of night work. The differential arose simply because men would not work at the low rates paid women inspectors, and it reflected a job market in which Corning could pay women less than men for the same work. That the company took advantage of such a situation may be understandable as a matter of economics, but its differential nevertheless became illegal once Congress enacted into law the principle of equal pay for equal work.

Did Corning Remedy Discrimination on Its Own?

We now must consider whether Corning continued to remain in violation of the Act after 1966 when, without changing the base wage rates for day and night inspectors, it began to permit women to bid for jobs on the night shift as vacancies occurred. It is evident that this was more than a token gesture to end discrimination, as turnover in the night shift inspection jobs was rapid. The record . . . shows, for example, that during the two-year period after June 1, 1966, the date women were first permitted to bid for night inspection jobs, women took 152 of the 278 openings, and women with very little seniority were able to obtain positions on the night shift. Relying on these facts, the company argues that it ceased discriminating against women in 1966, and was no longer in violation of the Equal Pay Act.

But the issue before us is not whether the company, in some abstract sense, can be said to have treated men the same as women after 1966. Rather, the question is whether the company remedied the specific violation of the Act which the Secretary proved. We agree with the Second Circuit, as well as with all other circuits that have had occasion to consider this issue, that the company could not cure its violation except by equalizing the base wages of female day inspectors with the higher rates paid the night inspectors. This result is implicit in the Act's language, its statement of purpose, and its legislative history.

As the Second Circuit noted, Congress enacted the Equal Pay Act "[r]ecognizing the weaker bargaining position of many women and believing that discrimination in wage rates represented unfair employer exploitation of this source of cheap labor." In response to evidence of the many families dependent on the income of working women, Congress included in the Act's statement of purpose a finding that "the existence . . . of wage differentials based on sex . . . depresses wages and living standards for employees necessary for their health and efficiency." And Congress declared it to be the policy of the Act to correct this condition.

Reducing Pay to Men Not a Legal Solution

To achieve this end, Congress required that employers pay equal pay for equal work and then specified:

> "Provided, That an employer who is paying a wage rate differential in violation of this subsection shall not, in order to comply with the provisions of this subsection, reduce the wage rate of any employee."

The purpose of this proviso was to ensure that to remedy violations of the Act, "[t]he lower wage rate must be increased to the level of the higher." Comments of individual legislators are all consistent with this view. Representative Dwyer remarked, for example, "The objective of equal pay legislation . . . is not to drag down men workers to the wage levels of women, but to raise women to the levels enjoyed by men in cases where discrimination is still practiced." Representative Griffin also thought it clear that "[t]he only way a violation could be remedied under the bill . . . is for the lower wages to be raised to the higher."

Allowing Women on Night Shift Not Full Compliance

By proving that after the effective date of the Equal Pay Act, Corning paid female day inspectors less than male night inspectors for equal work, the Secretary implicitly demonstrated that the wages of female day shift inspectors were unlawfully depressed and that the fair wage for inspection work was the base wage paid to male inspectors on the night shift. The whole purpose of the Act was to require that these depressed wages be raised, in part as a matter of simple justice to the employees themselves, but also as a matter of market economics, since Congress recognized as well that discrimination in wages on the basis of sex "constitutes an unfair method of competition."

We agree with Judge Friendly that

> "In light of this apparent congressional understanding, we cannot hold that Corning, by allowing some—or even many—women to move into the higher paid night jobs, achieved full compliance with the Act. Corning's action still left the inspectors on the day shift—virtually all women—earning a lower base wage than the night shift inspectors because of a differential initially based on sex and still not justified by any other consideration; in effect, Corning was still taking advantage of the availability of female labor to fill its day shift at a differentially low wage rate not justified by any factor other than sex."

The Equal Pay Act is broadly remedial, and it should be construed and applied so as to fulfill the underlying purposes which Congress sought to achieve. If, as the Secretary proved, the work performed by women on the day shift was equal to that performed by men on the night shift, the company became obligated to pay the women the same base wage as their male counterparts on the effective date of the Act. To permit the company to escape that obligation by agreeing to allow some women to work on the night shift at a higher rate of pay as vacancies occurred would frustrate, not serve, Congress' ends.

New Contract Gave No Retroactive Protection

The company's final contention—that it cured its violation of the Act when a new collective-bargaining agreement went into effect on January 20, 1969—need not detain us long. While the new agreement provided for equal base wages for night or day inspectors hired after that date, it continued to provide unequal base wages for employees hired before that date, a discrimination likely to continue for some time into the future because of a large number of laid-off employees who had to be offered re-employment before new inspectors could be hired. After considering the rather complex method in which the new wage rates for employees hired prior to January 1969 were calculated and the company's stated purpose behind the provisions of the new agreement, the District Court . . . concluded that the lower base wage for day inspectors was a direct product of the company's failure to equalize the base wages for male and female inspectors as of the effective date of the Act. We agree it is clear from the record that had the company equalized the base-wage rates of male and female inspectors on the effective date of the Act, as the law required, the day inspectors in 1969 would have been entitled to the same higher "red circle" rate the company provided for night inspectors. We therefore conclude that on the facts of this case, the company's continued discrimination in base wages between night and day workers, though phrased in terms of a

> "The primary criticism leveled at the
> EPA [Equal Pay Act] is that it has not
> eliminated the earnings disparity be-
> tween the sexes because it is applicable
> only to employment settings where men
> and women work in the same estab-
> lishment and perform substantially
> equal jobs."

Pay Inequity Between Men and Women

Susan Gluck Mezey

*Susan Gluck Mezey is a professor of political science and assis-
tant vice president for research at Loyola University in Chicago.*

*In the following selection Mezey maintains that the Equal Pay
Act, meant to provide "equal pay for equal work," has proven insufficient in closing the wage gap between men and women. According to Mezey the major limitation of the Act is that it applies only to employment settings in which both genders work in
the same establishment doing similar jobs. She further claims
that the Act fails to address a fundamental example of pay disparity in the workplace, evident in the fact that many jobs that
are typically occupied by females—such as the professions of
teacher, receptionist, and nurse—pay less than jobs commonly
dominated by males.*

Full-time women workers have always received less pay than
full-time men workers. In 1951, women earned only 63.9
cents for every dollar earned by men. Over the next four de-

Susan Gluck Mezey, *Elusive Equality: Women's Rights, Public Policy, and the Law*,
Boulder, CO: Lynne Rienner Publishers, 2003. Copyright © 2003 by Lynne Rienner
Publishers, Inc. All rights reserved. Reproduced by permission.

cades, the earnings gap between women and men fluctuated slightly, with women's earnings continuing to lag behind men's earnings. In 1992, the earnings gap finally began to narrow at a steady pace, albeit still slowly. But despite its positive movement, in that year, women still only earned 70 cents for every dollar men earned. And in 2000, notwithstanding almost forty years of equal pay legislation, the median weekly earnings for full-time women wage and salary workers were $491, 76 percent of the $646 earned by full-time men wage and salary workers. The wage gap varies with age, occupation, and race; generally, there is a smaller wage gap between the sexes among younger workers, but contrary to conventional wisdom, the gap does not decrease as women's salaries and wages rise. Among women aged forty-five to fifty-four, who had the highest earnings among women—$565—the gap widens, with women in this age group earning only 72.7 percent of men's median weekly earnings of $777.

The United States is not the only nation with pay disparity between the sexes; the gap exists throughout the world. "The inequality between women and men emerges as a 'global phenomenon'—a commonality eluding differences between women of various nations. No matter the nation women remain the least unionized and the lowest paid of all workers." There is evidence, however, that the European Union, through the legal interpretations of its European Court of Justice, has taken steps to remedy pay inequities between the sexes in the countries within its jurisdiction.

History of Equal Pay Efforts

The battle for pay equity in the United States dates back to the early part of the twentieth century, when just after World War I, Michigan and Montana adopted equal pay laws. The issue drew national attention in 1942, when the War Labor Board announced General Order No. 16, authorizing employers to pay equal wages to men and women employees "for comparable quality and quantity of work on the same or similar operations." During the 1960s, Esther Peterson, head of the Women's Bureau in the Department of Labor, spearheaded the drive for equal pay legislation. A presidential commission established by President [John F.] Kennedy in 1961 to assess pay imbalances recommended a comparable work bill, which was supported by the administration.

Pay equity proponents supported the Federal Equal Pay Act, encompassing an "equal pay for comparable work" standard because they feared that "equal work" would be interpreted as "identical work" and minor differences between jobs would be used to justify differentials in pay. During House debate over the bill, however, members of Congress objected that the standard of "equal pay for comparable work" was too far-reaching; they warned that employers would refuse to hire women at all if they had to pay them equal wages. Seeking to expedite its passage, Representative Katherine St. George, Republican of New York, offered an amendment that substituted the phrase "equal pay for equal work" for the proposed "equal pay for comparable work."

The substitution would have lasting legal and economic implications for women workers. Thus, despite its status as the first piece of national women's rights legislation, the law was less than a complete victory for women's rights advocates; when Congress was done, the narrow scope of the EPA seemed to ensure that it would encompass "only the most onerous offenses" of pay inequity. Signed by Kennedy on June 10, 1963, the EPA went into effect a year later on June 11, 1964. The act, requiring employers to pay men and women an equal salary for performing equal work, "marked the entrance of the federal government into the field of safeguarding the right of women to hold employment on the same basis as men." It was passed as an amendment to the Fair Labor Standards Act (FLSA) and was originally applicable only to workers covered by the FLSA. In 1972, Congress extended the EPA's provisions to executive, administrative, and professional employees. The FLSA Amendments of 1974 subsequently expanded equal pay protection to federal, state, and municipal workers. . . .

Interpretation of the Equal Pay Act

The EPA, which gave rise to the popular slogan "equal pay for equal work," bars employers from paying men and women in the same establishment differently

> for equal work on jobs, the performance of which requires equal skill, effort, and responsibility, and which are performed under similar working conditions, except where such payment is made pursuant to (i) a seniority system; (ii) a merit system; (iii) a system which measures earnings by quantity or quality of production; or (iv) a differential based on any other factor other than sex.

The act specifies that women's wages must be raised to match men's wages and that the latter cannot be lowered to the levels of women's wages. The secretary of labor was designated as the primary enforcement authority, but then in 1978, Carter's Civil Rights Reorganization Plan transferred responsibility for EPA enforcement to the EEOC; the transfer became effective on July 1, 1979.

To win an EPA suit, a plaintiff must show that an employee of the other sex is being paid higher wages for performing equal work. Although the act applies to either sex, the vast majority of suits are brought by or on behalf of women. Because Congress intended the law to remedy deep-seated wage disparities between men and women, the courts have only required plaintiffs to show that the jobs are "substantially equal," rather than identical. And once a plaintiff meets this test, the employer has an opportunity to show that the wage difference is based on one of the four reasons specified in the statute: merit, seniority, a difference in productivity, or "any other factor other than sex." The plaintiff bears the initial burden of proof of showing the wage difference, and the burden then shifts to the employer to prove that the differential is justified by one of the four exceptions permitted by the act. If the employer fails to satisfy the court that the wage differential is permitted by the act, that is, that it is not based on sex, then the plaintiff prevails without having to show a discriminatory motive on the part of the employer.

Substantially Equal Jobs

Schultz v. Wheaton Glass Company, a case decided in 1970, was the first appellate court opinion to construe the act, establishing the "substantially equal" test. In holding that jobs meriting equal pay need not be "identical" but only "substantially equal," the Third Circuit [of the U.S. Court of Appeals] paved the way for other circuits to construe the EPA, as it did, "as a broad charter of women's rights in the economic field"; ruling that Congress intended the Act to "overcome the age-old belief in women's inferiority and to eliminate the depressing effects on living standards of reduced wages for female workers and the economic and social consequences which flow from it."

This case demonstrates the importance of having the judiciary appraise the workers' duties rather than simply rely on the company's descriptions of the jobs performed by women and men. Because it was irrational to pay men twenty-one and a half cents an hour more than women for occasionally performing extra work—essentially unskilled labor—the court believed that the company's payment scheme was motivated by a desire to subordinate women. Noting that an economic benefit to the company might justify a pay differential, the court indicated that the company had not shown that the economic benefit was worth a 10 percent wage difference. Moreover, said the court, there was no reason why women could not perform the extra tasks to increase their value to the company and thereby merit the higher pay as well.

Skill, Effort, and Responsibility

Similarly, in *Hodgson v. Brookhaven General Hospital*, another 1970 ruling, the Fifth Circuit carefully examined the hospital's claim that its men orderlies were entitled to higher salaries than the women aides because the orderlies' jobs involved greater "skill, effort, and responsibility." The court outlined a test for assessing whether an employer's wage policy violates the act.

Conceding that orderlies and aides were at the same level of skill, effort, and responsibility in their primary jobs, the hospital argued that orderlies frequently performed additional tasks requiring greater skill, effort, and responsibility; moreover, the men were assigned to intimate jobs involving men patients. The trial court judge found and the appellate court concurred that the levels of skill and responsibility of the aides and orderlies were substantially equal and that the decisive issue was whether there was a difference in effort.

The circuit court explained that a difference in pay between jobs with overlapping duties is only justified if one job demands extra effort for a "significant amount" of time from all those performing the job and provides economic value to the employer in line with the pay difference. "Employers," the court continued, "may not be permitted to frustrate the purposes of the [Equal Pay] Act by calling for extra effort only occasionally, or only from one or two male employees."

The hospital argued that although orderlies and aides were responsible for approximately the same number of patients, orderlies were more frequently required to perform the non-routine patient care chores, and because of their extra effort, they deserved higher pay. Since the trial judge made no findings of fact on this crucial issue, the appellate court did not have the information necessary to rule on Brookhaven's defense. On remand, the trial court ruled against the hospital once more and ordered it to give the aides back pay and raise their salaries to match the orderlies' wages.

Any Other Factor Other than Sex

The ambiguously phrased exception to the EPA, "any other factor other than sex," has been the subject of more litigation than the other three exceptions combined. In *Hodgson v. Robert Hall Clothes*, a 1973 ruling, the Third Circuit articulated a definitive interpretation of this catch-all defense that has created a major obstacle for EPA plaintiffs to overcome when seeking relief under the act.

The secretary of labor filed suit against Robert Hall, a clothing store in Wilmington, Delaware. The suit alleged that the store paid its saleswomen, who sold women's clothes, less than its salesmen, who sold men's clothes, even though they performed equal work. The secretary argued that the "factor other than sex" phrase should not be construed as an open-ended invitation for pay disparity but should be limited to factors "related to job performance or . . . typically used in setting wage scales." The store contended that because men's clothes cost more, their department was more profitable and warranted higher pay for men. The circuit court agreed that the differential "economic benefit" to the employer was a "legitimate business reason" that vindicated the sex-based wage difference.

Congress had intended to allow employers to base wage differentials on job requirements or job performance measures only, and the Third Circuit's broad interpretation of the "other factor other than sex" exception in *Robert Hall* is at odds with the act's remedial purpose. By accepting the company's argument that the wage differential was justified because women provided less economic benefit to the company, the court ignored the fact that it was company policy that determined the respective economic benefits attributable to each sex. Additionally, in allowing Robert Hall to pay men more than women, the court accepted the policy of basing wages on the average earnings of the department as a whole, rather than on individual job performance. The court thus frustrated

Congress's intent in passing the EPA by permitting the company to justify the wage differential on the basis of its segregated workforce. Moreover, in accepting Robert Hall's "economic benefit" argument, the court opened the door to companies claiming market defense as a reason to evade the act. The lower federal courts have continued to interpret the "other than sex" defense so broadly that it has undermined women's ability to prove their equal pay claims.

The Supreme Court Rules on Equal Pay

Corning Glass Works v. Brennan was the first Equal Pay Act case to reach the Supreme Court. In this 1974 case, the Court was asked to determine whether men who worked on the night shift could be paid more than women who worked on the day shift.

Before 1925, only women inspected the finished glass products at the plant. Then, when it created a nighttime inspection shift, Corning hired men because women were barred from night work by New York State law. These new nighttime inspectors, men who transferred from higher-paying jobs within the plant, were paid more than the women daytime inspectors, even though their work was the same.

Aside from the inspecting jobs, there were no wage differences between nighttime and daytime workers until 1944, when the company established a pay differential between night and day work. The men inspectors, working at night, were able to add this extra increase to their already existing higher base pay. In 1966, Corning began to allow women to work at night and compete for the higher-paying night inspection jobs. Three years later, in 1969, the plant eliminated the day-night pay differential for inspectors hired after that year, yet the nighttime inspectors hired before 1969 continued to receive a higher wage that perpetuated the day-night wage distinction. In response to the EPA action against it, Corning argued that the wage differential between day and night work was permissible under the act as a "factor other than sex."

In a 5 to 3 vote, with Justice Thurgood Marshall announcing the decision, the Court explained that the EPA prohibits pay disparity for equal work in jobs performed under similar working conditions. Because the company's own job evaluation scheme indicated that working conditions differed by "surroundings" and "hazards," not by time of day, the differential pay for nighttime and daytime inspection jobs violated the EPA. Moreover, simply allowing women to become nighttime inspectors in 1966 had not cured the violation because men continued to receive higher wages than women for doing what the company's own evaluations showed was the same job; the only remedy was to raise the pay of the women day inspectors to the higher rates of the night inspectors. In rejecting the company's market defense, that is, the claim that women have historically worked for less pay, as a "factor other than sex," the Court signaled its intent to construe this affirmative defense narrowly; however, in subsequent cases, the lower courts have not always followed the high court in rejecting the market defense in EPA actions.

The EPA and State Employees

Recently, there has been concern that the Supreme Court's move toward "new federalism" during the 1990s would create an insurmountable obstacle for state employees who wished to bring EPA suits against state governments. "New federalism" refers to the Supreme Court's preference for enhancing state sovereignty over federal authority. The issue over the EPA arose as states defended themselves in EPA actions by arguing that the law failed to override the state's grant of immunity under the Eleventh Amendment of the U.S. Constitution. In the late 1990s, states had successfully claimed immunity in suits brought for age discrimination, discrimination on the basis of disability, and discrimination on the basis of family status. However, most lower federal courts that assessed the extent of the state's immunity under the act concluded that because the EPA was intended to prevent gender-based pay inequities, it was enacted under Congress's power to enforce the equal protection clause and did not exceed congressional authority to legislate against sex discrimination.

The Inadequacy of the EPA

Although women won millions of dollars in increased wages in EPA suits, the act's equal work requirement has meant that it "contribute[d] only modestly to closing the salary gap." Criticism of the EPA arises from two directions: one view, embodied in the writings of Richard Epstein and Richard Posner, argues that the EPA interferes with the free market, causing business inefficiencies and ultimately hurting the women it purports to benefit. However, the primary criticism leveled at the EPA is that it has not eliminated the earnings disparity between the sexes because it is applicable only to employment settings where men and women work in the same establishment and perform substantially equal jobs. It is of limited use, therefore, in a workforce consisting of sex-segregated occupations, that is, occupations predominantly (usually defined at about 70 percent) held by members of one sex.

The pervasiveness of sex segregation is illustrated by the fact that, in the early 1980s, over half of all women employed held clerical or service jobs. The oversupply of workers in the so-called pink-collar jobs—a term assigned to work typically dominated by women—depresses the wages of workers in those occupations. In 2000, almost 99 percent of all secretaries were women, as were more than 90 percent of registered nurses, nursing aides, receptionists, hairdressers, bookkeepers, and teacher's aides. Moreover, there were almost 100 occupations, including space scientists, dentists, architects, sheriffs, funeral directors, police officers, air traffic controllers, clergy, airline pilots, and motion picture projectionists, in which women constituted less than 25 percent of the workforce. It is very unlikely that women eschewed all jobs such as these, especially in light of evidence that they would substantially raise their earning capacity.

The severity of sex segregation in the workforce, which has been characterized as even more "widespread and more severe than racial discrimination," is the underlying basis for the theory known as comparable worth or pay equity. Beginning in the 1980s, women's rights advocates led the fight for comparable worth in the courts; their challenge was to reduce pay disparities in a highly sex-segregated workforce and stay within the bounds of acceptable legal theory.

"The wage gap expands to become a mommy gap for working mothers who are further penalized for their time out of the workforce to have children and their desire for more flexible hours."

The Promise of Equal Pay Has Not Come to Fruition

Cassandra Q. Butts

Cassandra Q. Butts is senior vice president for domestic policy at the Center for American Progress. Butts was a former senior advisor to Representative Richard A. Gephardt and served as the policy director on his 2004 presidential campaign. She is a recipient of the Georgetown Women's Law and Public Policy Fellowship, and a graduate of Harvard Law School and the University of North Carolina.

In the following essay Butts maintains that despite four decades of equal-pay legislation and litigation, women continue to earn significantly less than men, on average. Butts asserts that this disparity amounts to $200 billion annually. She describes the wage gap in detail and comments on the reasons for its persistence. Finally, Butts advocates possible solutions, including better enforcement of the Equal Pay Act and increased union representation for female workers.

The [2004] March for Women's Lives was by any measure a success in putting forward a comprehensive and progressive vision for the advancement of women's lives. One part of

Cassandra Q. Butts, "Marching On for Equal Pay," *www.americanprogress.org*, May 7, 2004. © Center for American Progress. This material was created by the Center for American Progress www.americanprogress.org.

that vision that deserves greater attention on this Mother's Day is the fight for economic equality.

Equal pay is an issue at the core of economic inequality for working women and their families across the nation. Since the passage of the Equal Pay Act in 1963, the promise of equal pay has been the law of the land. The Equal Pay Act made it illegal for employers to pay women a lower wage than men for the same job based on their gender. In fact, this year marks the 30th anniversary of the Supreme Court's 1974 ruling in *Corning Glass Works v. Brennan*, which affirmed the illegality of a wage differential based on gender.

Still, 41 years later, the promise of equal pay has not been fully realized and a persistent wage gap continues to exist between women and men. While the gap has narrowed since 1963, when women earned 59 percent of men's wages and this narrowing reflects the significant advancements women have made in the workplace, the most recent data indicates that women earned just 77 cents for every dollar earned by men in 2002.

The wage gap affects working women at every income level in the workforce. Whether in the professional ranks or the aisles of your local Wal-Mart, the wage gap knows no racial, ethnic or geographic boundaries.

The wage gap expands to become a mommy gap for working mothers who are further penalized for their time out of the workforce to have children and their desire for more flexible hours. It is estimated that a first child lowers earnings for a mother by 7.5 percent, while a second child lowers her earnings by another 8 percent.

For working women and their families, the wage gap amounts to $200 billion annually in lost income. For the average 25-year old working woman, the wage gap will amount to $523,000 in lost wages during her lifetime. To put that number into perspective, the average lifetime benefit for getting a college education is $1,000,000 in additional earnings. And beyond our working lives, the income lost from the wage gap results in greater retirement insecurity for women through smaller pensions.

While the wage gap affects all working women and their families, it more significantly narrows the economic opportunities available to women of color. African-American women earn just 68 cents of every dollar earned by men, and Latinas far even worse by earning just 56 cents. Because higher percentages of African-American women and Latinas lead single-parent families (49.7 percent of African-American families and 21 percent of Hispanic families compared to 15.5 percent of white families), the wage gap is one of several factors contributing to the higher rates of poverty among women of color and their families.

Instead of moving forward on the constructive path of enforcing and strengthening the Equal Pay Act, the Bush administration has taken affirmative steps to deter enforcement. The Department of Labor has effectively ended the Equal Pay Matters Initiative, a Clinton-era effort designed to provide working women with the information and resources needed to compete with men in the workplace. The Labor Department Web site has been wiped clean of any reference to the wage gap, as if it never existed. And the Bush administration continues to push potentially crippling reform of the overtime pay system that could cost working women millions of dollars in lost wages.

The most obvious solution to closing the wage gap is strengthening enforcement of the Equal Pay Act. One such legislative effort, the Paycheck Fairness Act, seeks to do so by closing loopholes in the existing law that weaken its effectiveness as a tool for ending sex discrimination in wages. The Paycheck Fairness Act would strengthen the remedies provision of the act in three important ways: it will allow prevailing plaintiffs to recover compensatory and punitive damages; make it easier to bring class-action lawsuits on behalf of groups of women; and improve the collection of wage data by the Equal Employment Opportunity Commission, thereby enhancing the agency's ability to determine whether violations of the law are taking place.

In addition to the Paycheck Fairness Act, there are other important policy proposals that address the problem of lower wages in occupations dominated by women. One policy that deserves attention would allow lawsuits to be filed under the Civil Rights Act of 1964 when women are paid less than men in comparable jobs.

Another effective tool for closing the wage gap is to expand unionization of the workforce. Working women who have union representation earn 33 percent more than women who are not union members. Proposals such as the Employee Right To Choose Act would protect the rights of workers to organize and further the cause of equal pay.

As we. . . take the next steps towards advancing the agenda of the March for Women's Lives, we owe our working mothers, and all women, a renewed focus on achieving economic equality.

CHAPTER 3

Sexual Harassment

Case Overview

Meritor Savings Bank
v. Vinson (1986)

In *Meritor Savings Bank v. Vinson*, the U.S. Supreme Court ruled that an employer may be held liable for sexual harassment under civil rights laws when an employee is subjected to a "hostile environment," even when the employee suffered no direct economic loss from the harassment. The case helped bring public attention to the issue of sexual harassment in the workplace and prompted a flood of complaints and litigation against employers.

A situation in which an employee faces the loss of a job, lost opportunities for promotion, or other economic detriment for refusing a supervisor's sexual advances—or one in which the employee is offered preferential treatment in exchange for sex—is known in legal terms as *quid pro quo* (one thing exchanged for another) sexual harassment. Courts had previously recognized that an employee may use civil rights laws to recover damages for this type of harassment. *Meritor*, however, was the first Supreme Court case to establish that civil rights laws are broad enough to cover a different type of sexual harassment, that involving a hostile work environment. In a hostile-environment case, an employee faces no job-related economic loss or benefit based on performing sexual favors. Instead, the employee's claim is grounded on having been subjected to a pattern of humiliating or frightening sexual conduct at work.

Meritor was a lawsuit brought by a former employee who alleged that her supervisor at the bank had sexually harassed her for four years. She claimed that the harassment was a violation of Title VII of the Civil Rights Act of 1964. At trial in federal district court, the former employee testified that she was pressured by the supervisor to enter into a sexual relationship with him, although she acknowledged that she was not threatened with the loss of her job or any other penalty. The supervisor then subjected the employee to numerous instances of often-flagrant sexual harassment on and off the job, she claimed. The supervisor flatly denied the allegations and the bank contended it had no knowledge of the alleged harassment while it was taking place. The district court ruled against the former employee, stating that if a sexual relationship indeed existed, it was voluntary and did not result in her losing her job, being denied promotions, or experiencing other economic loss. Thus, the court concluded that the former employee had not been a victim of the *quid pro quo* harassment then recognized as the sole basis for liability. The court further found that the bank itself would not have been liable for the supervisor's actions anyway, as the alleged misconduct had not been reported to bank management.

A federal court of appeals reversed the district court's ruling, and the U.S. Supreme Court accepted the case for review. The Supreme Court held that the existence of a "hostile environment"—for example, an office setting in which an employee is repeatedly subjected to requests for sexual favors or sexually explicit remarks—indeed violates Title VII, even if the harassment does not result in economic loss by the employee. The Court further held that even if an employee voluntarily enters into a sexual relationship with a supervisor, that fact does not entitle the supervisor to subject the employee to sexual harassment. The key issue, the Court ruled, was whether the particular incidents of sexual harassment complained about by the employee were "unwelcome." The Court acknowledged, however, that evidence of an employee's sexually provocative speech or dress could be admitted as evidence in the supervisor's defense if it related to the issue of whether the supervisor's conduct was unwelcome. In a concurring opinion, four of the Supreme Court justices stated that a company employing a supervisor who had sexually harassed a subordinate employee could be directly liable for the misconduct even if the harassment had not been reported to the company, with some exceptions.

Meritor began an era in which sexual harassment became a common and hotly debated topic in American society. Five years later, the Anita Hill–Clarence Thomas incident brought further attention to the issue. Hill was a former employee of Thomas, who had been nominated to the U.S. Supreme Court in 1991. During Senate hearings on confirmation of Thomas as the next Supreme Court justice, Hill testified that Thomas had sexually harassed her. Thomas denied the accusations, and his confirmation to the Court was narrowly approved by Congress. Official complaints of sexual harassment skyrocketed after the *Meritor* case. In 1985, the year before *Meritor* was decided, the federal Equal Employment Opportunity Commission received an average of fewer than ten charges of sexual harassment per year. In 1986 the Commission received 624 complaints. By 1995 annual complaints neared 5,000, although the number leveled off thereafter.

Legal protection against sexual harassment has improved in the two decades since *Meritor*. However, legal commentators note that significant obstacles remain for harassment victims. Subsequent court decisions have made it easier for employers to defend against harassment claims by establishing procedures under which employees are required to immediately report harassing acts. However, research has shown that reporting requirements actually deter many employees from reporting harassment, out of embarrassment and fear of retaliation.

> *"Respondent's allegations in this case—*
> *which include not only pervasive ha-*
> *rassment but also criminal conduct of*
> *the most serious nature—are plainly*
> *sufficient to state a claim for 'hostile*
> *environment' sexual harassment."*

The Court's Decision: "Hostile Environment" Claims Can Constitute Sexual Harassment and Thus Violate Title VII

Justice William Rehnquist

Justice William H. Rehnquist was born on October 1, 1924, in Milwaukee, Wisconsin. He earned undergraduate and postgraduate degrees from Stanford University and Harvard University before enrolling at Stanford Law School, from which he graduated in 1952. Justice Rehnquist served as assistant attorney general for the Office of Legal Counsel in the Department of Justice before he was appointed to the U.S. Supreme Court by President Richard M. Nixon in 1971. In 1986 he was named Chief Justice of the United States by President Ronald Reagan. Rehnquist served on the Court until his death in 2005 at the age of eighty.

In the 1986 case Meritor Savings Bank v. Vinson, *the U.S. Supreme Court ruled that an employee may successfully sue for sexual harassment if the workplace presents a "hostile environment," even if the worker suffers no economic loss. In the following excerpt from the majority opinion written by Justice*

Justice William Rehnquist, majority opinion, *Meritor Savings Bank v. Vinson*, 477 U.S. 57, 1986.

Rehnquist, the Court determined that an employer may be held liable for sexual harassment even if the employee was voluntarily involved in a sexual relationship with the supervisor who committed the harassment. One of the key issues in the Court's decision was whether sexual advances in the workplace were "unwelcome." However, the Court added that evidence of sexually provocative speech or dress on the part of the employee claiming harassment may be admitted at trial as part of the employer's defense.

Title VII of the Civil Rights Act of 1964 makes it "an unlawful employment practice for an employer . . . to discriminate against any individual with respect to his compensation, terms, conditions, or privileges of employment, because of such individual's race, color, religion, sex, or national origin." The prohibition against discrimination based on sex was added to Title VII at the last minute on the floor of the House of Representatives. The principal argument in opposition to the amendment was that "sex discrimination" was sufficiently different from other types of discrimination that it ought to receive separate legislative treatment. This argument was defeated, the bill quickly passed as amended, and we are left with little legislative history to guide us in interpreting the Act's prohibition against discrimination based on "sex."

Respondent argues, and the Court of Appeals held, that unwelcome sexual advances that create an offensive or hostile working environment violate Title VII. Without question, when a supervisor sexually harasses a subordinate because of the subordinate's sex, that supervisor "discriminate[s]" on the basis of sex. Petitioner apparently does not challenge this proposition. It contends instead that in prohibiting discrimination with respect to "compensation, terms, conditions, or privileges" of employment, Congress was concerned with what petitioner describes as "tangible loss" of "an economic character," not "purely psychological aspects of the workplace environment." In support of this claim petitioner observes that in both the legislative history of Title VII and this Court's Title VII decisions, the focus has been on tangible, economic barriers erected by discrimination.

Expanding Antiharassment Protection

We reject petitioner's view. First, the language of Title VII is not limited to "economic" or "tangible" discrimination. The phrase "terms, conditions, or privileges of employment" evinces a congressional intent "'to strike at the entire spectrum of disparate treatment of men and women'" in employment. Petitioner has pointed to nothing in the Act to suggest that Congress contemplated the limitation urged here.

Second, in 1980 the EEOC [U.S. Equal Employment Opportunity Commission] issued Guidelines specifying that "sexual harassment," as there defined, is a form of sex discrimination prohibited by Title VII. As an "administrative interpretation of the Act by the enforcing agency," these Guidelines, "'while not controlling upon the courts by reason of their authority, do constitute a body of experience and informed judgment to which courts and litigants may properly resort for guidance.'" The EEOC Guidelines fully support the view that harassment leading to noneconomic injury can violate Title VII.

In defining "sexual harassment," the Guidelines first describe the kinds of workplace conduct that may be actionable under Title VII. These include "[u]nwelcome sexual advances, requests for sexual favors, and other verbal or physical conduct of a sexual nature." Relevant to the charges at issue in this case, the Guidelines provide that such sexual misconduct constitutes prohibited "sexual harassment," whether or not it is directly linked to the grant or denial of an economic quid pro quo [one thing exchanged for another], where "such conduct has the purpose or effect of unreasonably interfering with an individual's work performance or creating an intimidating, hostile, or offensive working environment."

Prohibiting "Hostile Environment" at Work

In concluding that so-called "hostile environment" (i. e., non quid pro quo) harassment violates Title VII, the EEOC drew upon a substantial body of judicial decisions and EEOC precedent holding that Title VII affords employees the right to work in an environment free from discriminatory intimidation, ridicule, and insult. *Rogers v. EEOC*, 1971 was apparently the first case to recognize a cause of action based upon a discriminatory work environment. In *Rogers* the Court of Appeals for the Fifth Circuit held that a Hispanic complainant could establish a Title VII violation by demonstrating that her employer created an offensive work environment for employees by giving discriminatory service to its Hispanic clientele. The court explained that an employee's protections under Title VII extend beyond the economic aspects of employment:

> "[T]he phrase 'terms, conditions or privileges of employment' in [Title VII] is an expansive concept which sweeps within its protective ambit the practice of creating a working environment heavily charged with ethnic or racial discrimination. . . . One can readily envision working environments so heavily polluted with discrimination as to destroy completely the emotional and psychological stability of minority group workers. . . ."

Courts applied this principle to harassment based on race, and national origin. Nothing in Title VII suggests that a hostile environment based on discriminatory sexual harassment should not be likewise prohibited. The Guidelines thus appropriately drew from, and were fully consistent with, the existing case law.

Comparison Made to Racist Atmosphere

Since the Guidelines were issued, courts have uniformly held, and we agree, that a plaintiff may establish a violation of Title VII by proving that discrimination based on sex has created a hostile or abusive work environment. As the Court of Appeals for the Eleventh Circuit wrote in *Henson v. Dundee*, (1982):

> "Sexual harassment which creates a hostile or offensive environment for members of one sex is every bit the arbitrary barrier to sexual equality at the workplace that racial harassment is to racial equality. Surely, a requirement that a man or woman run a gauntlet of sexual abuse in return for the privilege of being allowed to work and make a living can be as demeaning and disconcerting as the harshest of racial epithets."

Of course, as the courts in both *Rogers* and *Henson* recognized, not all workplace conduct that may be described as "harassment" affects a "term, condition, or privilege" of employment within the meaning of Title VII. For sexual harassment to be actionable, it must be sufficiently severe or pervasive "to alter the conditions of [the victim's] employment and create an abusive working environment." Respondent's allegations in this case—which include not only pervasive harassment but also criminal conduct of the most serious nature—are plainly sufficient to state a claim for "hostile environment" sexual harassment.

Whether Unwelcome Sexual Advances are Key

The question remains, however, whether the District Court's ultimate finding that respondent "was not the victim of sexual harassment" effectively disposed of respondent's claim. The Court of Appeals recognized, we think correctly, that this ultimate finding was likely based on one or both of two erroneous views of the law. First, the District Court apparently believed that a claim for sexual harassment will not lie absent an economic effect on the complainant's employment. Since it appears that the District Court made its findings without ever considering the "hostile environment" theory of sexual harassment, the Court of Appeals' decision to remand was correct.

Second, the District Court's conclusion that no actionable harassment occurred might have rested on its earlier "finding" that "[i]f [respondent] and Taylor did engage in an intimate or sexual relationship . . . , that relationship was a voluntary one." But the fact that sex-ralated conduct was "voluntary," in the sense that the complainant was not forced to participate against her will, is not a defense to a sexual harassment suit brought under Title VII. The gravamen [the significant part of the grievance] of any sexual harassment claim is that the alleged sexual advances were "unwelcome." While the question whether particular conduct was indeed unwelcome presents difficult problems of proof and turns largely on credibility determinations committed to the trier of fact, the District Court in this case erroneously focused on the "voluntariness" of respondent's participation in the claimed sexual episodes. The correct inquiry is whether respondent by her conduct indicated that the alleged sexual advances were unwelcome, not whether her actual participation in sexual intercourse was voluntary.

Evidence of Provocative Speech and Dress May Be Admissible

Petitioner contends that even if this case must be remanded to the District Court, the Court of Appeals erred in one of the terms of its remand. Specifically, the Court of Appeals stated that testimony about respondent's "dress and personal fantasies," which the District Court apparently admitted into evidence, "had no place in this litigation." The apparent ground for this conclusion was that respondent's voluntariness vel non [or not] in submitting to Taylor's advances was immaterial to her sexual harassment claim. While "voluntariness" in the sense of consent is not a defense to such a claim, it does not follow that a complainant's sexually provocative speech or dress is irrelevant as a matter of law in determining whether he or she found particular sexual advances unwelcome. To the contrary, such evidence is obviously relevant. The EEOC Guidelines emphasize that the trier of fact must determine the existence of sexual harassment in light of "the record as a whole" and "the totality of circumstances, such as the nature of the sexual advances and the context in which the alleged incidents occurred." Respondent's claim that any marginal relevance of the evidence in question was outweighed by the potential for unfair prejudice is the sort of argument properly addressed to the District Court. In this case the District Court concluded that the evidence should be admitted, and the Court of Appeals' contrary conclusion was based upon the erroneous, categorical view that testimony about provocative dress and publicly expressed sexual fantasies "had no place in this litigation." While the District Court must carefully weigh the applicable considerations in deciding whether to admit evidence of this kind, there is no per se rule against its admissibility. . . .

In sum, we hold that a claim of "hostile environment" sex discrimination is actionable under Title VII, that the District Court's findings were insufficient to dispose of respondent's hostile environment claim, and that the District Court did not err in admitting testimony about respondent's sexually provocative speech and dress. As to employer liability, we conclude that the Court of Appeals was wrong to entirely disregard agency principles and impose absolute liability on employers for the acts of their supervisors, regardless of the circumstances of a particular case.

Accordingly, the judgment of the Court of Appeals reversing the judgment of the District Court is affirmed, and the case is remanded for further proceedings consistent with this opinion.

> "It is precisely because the supervisor is understood to be clothed with the employer's authority that he is able to impose unwelcome sexual conduct on subordinates."

Concurring Opinion: Employers are Liable for the Sexual Harassment of an Employee by a Supervisor

Justice Thurgood Marshall

Justice Thurgood Marshall was born in 1908 in Baltimore, Maryland. In 1933 he graduated from Howard University Law School in Washington, D.C. For over twenty years, Justice Marshall fought racial segregation through his legal work with the NAACP (National Association for the Advancement of Colored People). He argued the U.S. Supreme Court case of Brown v. Board of Education *in 1954, and was assigned to the United States Court of Appeals for the Second Circuit in 1961. Justice Marshall was appointed to the U.S. Supreme Court by President Lyndon B. Johnson in 1967. He served on the Court until 1991 and died two years later at the age of eighty-four.*

The following article is an excerpt from the concurring opinion in Meritor Savings Bank v. Vinson, *the U.S. Supreme Court case that was decided in 1986. As author of the concurrence, Justice Marshall elaborates on the issue of an employer's legal liability for sexual harassment committed by a supervisor against a*

Justice Thurgood Marshall, concurring opinion, *Meritor Savings Bank v. Vinson*, 477 U.S. 57, 1986.

subordinate employee. Marshall affirms that an employer is liable for a manager's intimidation of a coworker in "hostile environment" cases, even if the employer had no prior knowledge of the manager's misconduct.

I fully agree with the Court's conclusion that workplace sexual harassment is illegal, and violates Title VII [of the Civil Rights Act of 1964].... The Court's opinion, however, leaves open the circumstances in which an employer is responsible under Title VII for such conduct. Because I believe that question to be properly before us, I write separately.

The issue the Court declines to resolve is addressed in the EEOC [U.S. Equal Employment Opportunity Commission] Guidelines on Discrimination Because of Sex, which are entitled to great deference [citations omitted throughout]. The Guidelines explain:

> "Applying general Title VII principles, an employer ... is responsible for its acts and those of its agents and supervisory employees with respect to sexual harassment regardless of whether the specific acts complained of were authorized or even forbidden by the employer and regardless of whether the employer knew or should have known of their occurrence. The Commission will examine the circumstances of the particular employment relationship and the job [f]unctions performed by the individual in determining whether an individual acts in either a supervisory or agency capacity.

> "With respect to conduct between fellow employees, an employer is responsible for acts of sexual harassment in the workplace where the employer (or its agents or supervisory employees) knows or should have known of the conduct, unless it can show that it took immediate and appropriate corrective action."

Employer Liable for Harassment by Supervisors

The Commission, in issuing the Guidelines, explained that its rule was "in keeping with the general standard of employer li-

ability with respect to agents and supervisory employees. . . .
[T]he Commission and the courts have held for years that an
employer is liable if a supervisor or an agent violates the Title
VII, regardless of knowledge or any other mitigating factor." I
would adopt the standard set out by the Commission.

An employer can act only through individual supervisors
and employees; discrimination is rarely carried out pursuant
to a formal vote of a corporation's board of directors. Although an employer may sometimes adopt companywide discriminatory policies violative of Title VII, acts that may constitute Title VII violations are generally effected through the
actions of individuals, and often an individual may take such
a step even in defiance of company policy. Nonetheless, Title
VII remedies, such as reinstatement and backpay, generally
run against the employer as an entity. The question thus arises
as to the circumstances under which an employer will be held
liable under Title VII for the acts of its employees.

The answer supplied by general Title VII law, like that
supplied by federal labor law, is that the act of a supervisory
employee or agent is imputed [legally attributed] to the employer. Thus, for example, when a supervisor discriminatorily
fires or refuses to promote a black employee, that act is, without more, considered the act of the employer. The courts do
not stop to consider whether the employer otherwise had "notice" of the action, or even whether the supervisor had actual
authority to act as he did. Following that approach, every
Court of Appeals that has considered the issue has held that
sexual harassment by supervisory personnel is automatically
imputed to the employer when the harassment results in tangible job detriment to the subordinate employee.

Employer Liability Includes Hostile Environment

The brief filed by the Solicitor General on behalf of the United
States and the EEOC in this case suggests that a different rule

should apply when a supervisor's harassment "merely" results in a discriminatory work environment. The Solicitor General concedes that sexual harassment that affects tangible job benefits is an exercise of authority delegated to the supervisor by the employer, and thus gives rise to employer liability. But, departing from the EEOC Guidelines, he argues that the case of a supervisor merely creating a discriminatory work environment is different because the supervisor "is not exercising, or threatening to exercise, actual or apparent authority to make personnel decisions affecting the victim." In the latter situation, he concludes, some further notice requirement should therefore be necessary.

The Solicitor General's position is untenable. A supervisor's responsibilities do not begin and end with the power to hire, fire, and discipline employees, or with the power to recommend such actions. Rather, a supervisor is charged with the day-to-day supervision of the work environment and with ensuring a safe, productive workplace. There is no reason why abuse of the latter authority should have different consequences than abuse of the former. In both cases it is the authority vested in the supervisor by the employer that enables him to commit the wrong: it is precisely because the supervisor is understood to be clothed with the employer's authority that he is able to impose unwelcome sexual conduct on subordinates. There is therefore no justification for a special rule, to be applied only in "hostile environment" cases, that sexual harassment does not create employer liability until the employee suffering the discrimination notifies other supervisors. No such requirement appears in the statute, and no such requirement can coherently be drawn from the law of agency.

Agency principles and the goals of Title VII law make appropriate some limitation on the liability of employers for the acts of supervisors. Where, for example, a supervisor has no authority over an employee, because the two work in wholly different parts of the employer's business, it may be improper to find strict employer liability. Those considerations, however, do not justify the creation of a special "notice" rule in hostile environment cases.

No Requirement That Employer Have Notice

Further, nothing would be gained by crafting such a rule. In the "pure" hostile environment case, where an employee files an EEOC complaint alleging sexual harassment in the workplace, the employee seeks not money damages but injunctive relief. Under Title VII, the EEOC must notify an employer of charges made against it within 10 days after receipt of the complaint. If the charges appear to be based on "reasonable cause," the EEOC must attempt to eliminate the offending practice through "informal methods of conference, conciliation, and persuasion." An employer whose internal procedures assertedly would have redressed the discrimination can avoid injunctive relief by employing these procedures after receiving notice of the complaint or during the conciliation period. Where a complainant, on the other hand, seeks backpay on the theory that a hostile work environment effected a constructive termination, the existence of an internal complaint procedure may be a factor in determining not the employer's liability but the remedies available against it. Where a complainant without good reason bypassed an internal complaint procedure she knew to be effective, a court may be reluctant to find constructive termination and thus to award reinstatement or backpay.

I therefore reject the Solicitor General's position. I would apply in this case the same rules we apply in all other Title VII cases and hold that sexual harassment by a supervisor of an employee under his supervision, leading to a discriminatory work environment, should be imputed to the employer for Title VII purposes regardless of whether the employee gave "notice" of the offense.

> *"The story of* Meritor Savings Bank v.
> Vinson *and its aftermath illustrates
> how deeply involved the Supreme Court
> and lower courts have been in the evo-
> lution of gender relations."*

The Legacy of Sexual Harassment Rulings

Augustus B. Cochran III

*Augustus B. Cochran III is a professor of political science at
Agnes Scott College in Decatur, Georgia. He earned a PhD from
the University of North Carolina at Chapel Hill, and also holds
a law degree. He is affiliated with a labor law firm in Atlanta.*

Meritor Savings Bank v. Vinson *increased public awareness of
sexual harassment and set in motion a flurry of harassment lawsuits that have had a significant impact on gender relations over
the past twenty years. In the following selection Cochran assesses
the social influence of the case as well as its impact on the enforcement of sexual harassment law. He also considers the limitations of enforcement given the burden placed on the victim to
report discrimination and the tendency of many women to respond less aggressively.*

The social impact of Supreme Court decisions is controversial, and adding sexual harassment to the mix merely am-
plifies the controversy. Whether to use law to reform social
mores and structures, the extent to which laws alter practices
and patterns of society, and the benefits of legally restructur-
ing social relations are all disputed issues. . . .

Augustus B. Cochran III, *Sexual Harassment and the Law: The Mechelle Vinson Case*,
pp. 166–90, Lawrence, KS: University Press of Kansas, 2004. Copyright © 2004 by the
University Press of Kansas. All rights reserved. Reproduced by permission.

The Supreme Court's Influence

Although no assessment of the impact of *Vinson* and its progeny can be definitive, if for no other reason than the battle against sexual harassment is an ongoing rather than a completed campaign, one predictable result of the Court's speaking on an issue is to heighten public attention. In shining the spotlight of press and public opinion on an issue, a Supreme Court decision may not finally settle the dispute so much as set in motion other influences that more decisively affect the outcome, possibly years later. The Supreme Court's agenda-setting role can be seen as a precondition for change, affecting which actors play leading roles in the resolution process. Supreme Court decisions also frame the terms of debate, and legal doctrines and concepts shape the way we think. Both by expanding the scope of involvement through increased visibility and by defining the terms of debate, Supreme Court decisions profoundly shape the politics of change.

International Approaches
to Sexual Harassment Law

Supreme Court rulings and American legal doctrines have international repercussions as well. As Margaret Crouch observes, "While the United States has led the world in recognition of sexual harassment as a phenomenon and development of the concept of sexual harassment, other countries have been quick to follow." A 1992 survey of twenty-three industrialized countries by the International Labor Organization found that only seven had statutes that specifically addressed sexual harassment, but judicial decisions in six others, including the United States, explicitly dealt with the offense. In most other nations, the law prohibited sexual harassment by implication as a violation of other legal strictures, such as unjust discharge, torts, or criminal law. Canada, Great Britain, and Australia have hewn most closely to the U.S. path, defining sexual harassment as sex discrimination. Other nations have enacted alternative approaches. Spain treats the offense as an invasion of privacy. France criminalizes sexual harassment but narrows the scope of the offense to include only quid pro quo harassment and to exclude harassment by coworkers. International organizations are another source of legal prohibitions. The United Nations, International Labor Organization, and European Community have condemned sexual harassment, and the UN's Commission on the Status of Women classified it as violence against women. Although Crouch finds that U.S. sexual harassment law has exercised widespread influence, she concludes that American law is more moralistic, with a tendency for some interpretations to emphasize sexual misconduct rather than gender discrimination. Alternative approaches de-emphasize gender, instead banning discrimination and sexual harassment as violations of employee rights and the dignity of all humans.

Legal Impact:
Enforcing Sexual Harassment Law

Although expectations, and certainly hopes, are that authoritative statements by law-giving bodies will have a significant and salutary effect in curbing misconduct, assessing the effects of one case or of legal changes in general apart from other political, social, and economic factors is difficult if not impossible. Not surprisingly, statistical data measuring the direct impact that *Vinson* and sexual harassment law have had on sexually harassing conduct are lacking. Countervailing factors make increased reporting of incidents likely, even if the actual amount of misconduct has declined. Higher visibility doubtless raises awareness, encouraging more resistance, including complaints. Certainly sexual harassment has moved to center stage in our legal, business, educational, and political institutions as complaints have grown and highly publicized cases have captured the public's imagination and stirred whirling controversies about efficacy and legitimacy of sexual harassment law in the post-*Vinson* era.

Sexual Harassment After *Vinson*

Charges of sexual harassment grew exponentially in the years after *Vinson*. The Equal Employment Opportunity Commission registered fewer than 10 charges per year before 1986; that year, the number catapulted to 624, climbing steadily to 2,217 in 1990 and to 4,626 in 1995. Since the mid-1990s, however, filings leveled off, with 4,783 filings in 1999, accounting for 6.2 percent of the almost 80,000 employment discrimination charges recorded by the agency. Combining EEOC charges and those filed with state fair employment practices agencies, a similar pattern occurs: 10,532 sexual harassment charges were filed in 1992, increasing by roughly 50 percent to 15,549 in the next five years, but growing slowly thereafter; 15,836 charges were filed with state and federal antidiscrimination agencies in 2000. Males are filing a growing proportion of the charges: 9.1 percent in 1992, and 13.6 percent in 2000. EEOC data do not report whether these charges were lodged against females or other males.

Agencies pursued 28.2 percent of these charges to "merit resolutions." Resolutions included finding reasonable cause to believe that discrimination had occurred, typically followed by attempts to conciliate the parties (successful in 3.1 percent and unsuccessful in 6.8 percent of the cases), negotiated settlements (10 percent of the time), or withdrawal with benefits (covering the 8.3 percent of cases in which the complaining party withdrew the charge upon receipt of the desired benefits). The average amount of compensation that agencies won for persons charging sexual harassment doubled from 1996 to 2000. In 1992, the aggregate amount of monetary benefits recouped was $12.7 million; charging parties received $54.6 million in 2000. Agencies closed 27.7 percent of the cases on various administrative grounds, including that the charging party withdrew the charge or failed to pursue the case. No reasonable cause to believe discrimination had occurred was determined in 44.1 percent of the cases, although the charging parties could bring private lawsuits despite being unsuccessful before the EEOC.

The Growth of Sexual Harassment Lawsuits

In federal courts, sexual harassment cases have been a substantial part of the colossal growth in employment lawsuits. The number of employment cases, most claiming discrimination, has increased more than 430 percent since the early 1970s. By 1996, there were 23,000 court cases alleging employment discrimination, double the number of filings in 1992, and the trend was for the number to increase by 20 percent annually. By 2002, the *Economist* reported that one out of five civil cases in the United States involved harassment or discrimination, compared with one in twenty a decade ago, and the Administrative Office of the Courts reported that employment discrimination cases were approaching 10 percent of the federal docket.

Sexual harassment lawsuits increased from fewer than 7,000 to about 18,000 during the 1990s. A study by Ann Juliano and Stewart J. Schwab uncovered 650 sexual harassment cases with reported opinions in the federal district and appeals courts in the decade after the *Vinson* decision. The authors recognize that by eliminating cases that did not result in a reported opinion by a judge, they are studying cases high up in the naming-blaming-claiming pyramid, possibly skewing their sample toward overrepresenting more serious and meritorious claims. Probably 95 percent of cases, like *Vinson* settle out of court, and most court cases do not produce reported decisions. Nonetheless, the study yields the most comprehensive overview available of judicial enforcement of sexual harassment law after *Vinson*.

Demographics

Partially reported demographic data indicate that males accounted for 5.4 percent of the plaintiffs. Plaintiffs tended to mirror the population in their marital and occupational status: most plaintiffs were blue collar (38 percent) or clerical (29 percent); professionals were slightly underrepresented, but managers were somewhat overrepresented, among plaintiffs. Eighty-nine percent had quit before suing. Individuals rather than government agencies, advocacy organizations, or class actions brought virtually all suits.

Mixed male-female workplaces accounted for about two-thirds of the cases, and about one-third involved mostly male workplaces. A negligible number of cases involved predominantly female workplaces. Almost one-fourth of the alleged misconduct occurred off-premises, although about half of these cases resulted from employment-related events, such as company parties. The remainder was divided almost equally between private socializing, such as after-hours drinks, and nonconsensual conduct, such as calls or visits to the victim's home. Most lawsuits were against private employers, but the federal government was the defendant in 4 percent of the cases and state and local governments in 23 percent (roughly twice the proportion of the labor force comprising these government employees).

Statistics of Sexual Harassment Suits

About 70 percent exclusively charged hostile environment harassment; another 22.5 percent combined hostile environment with quid pro quo claims. Pure quid pro quo cases represented only 7.5 percent of the sample. Male-dominated workplaces were more likely to generate hostile environment claims. Clerical and blue-collar plaintiffs were more likely to complain of physical harassment (50 and 48 percent, respectively) than were professionals (38 percent) or managers (32 percent). Most sexual harassment was directed at the plaintiff specifically and was not based on comments about women in general or diffuse material such as pinups or posters (7 percent). Only 4 percent of the cases involved a single incident, and plaintiffs prevailed at a lower rate (35 percent) in these suits. Despite the passage of the Civil Rights Act of 1991, only twenty-nine of these cases from 1986 to 1996 were tried before juries (including only three of the thirty-three cases covered by the 1991 act). The authors detected a trend for judges to act as gatekeepers by dismissing plaintiffs' claims based on legal conclusions before airing factual contentions at trial. Only about one-third of the cases went to trial, but when they did, plaintiffs did significantly better before a jury than in a bench trial.

Female plaintiffs fared better than males, and blue-collar and clerical plaintiffs were more successful than professionals and managers. Plaintiffs' success rates rose if both supervisors and coworkers participated in the harassment, and greater numbers of harassers increased the likelihood of plaintiff victory. Plaintiffs were likely to prevail when sexual comments (57 percent win rate) or derogatory comments (59 percent) were directed specifically at them, although without some physical component to the harassment, plaintiffs' win rate fell to 45 percent. When companies had no formal sexual harassment programs or grievance procedures, plaintiffs won 71 percent of their cases. When plaintiffs had not complained, however, they lost almost 70 percent of the time. Overall, plaintiffs and defendants won about half the time in district court, but plaintiffs appealed more often, 74 percent of the cases; employers filed 18 percent of the appeals, and both parties appealed in 8 percent of the decisions. On appeal, plaintiffs and defendants were equally unsuccessful, each winning reversals in 27 percent of the cases.

Compensation Awards

During this period, plaintiff win rates rose from 40 percent in 1986, the year of the *Vinson* decision, to 55.2 percent in 1995.

More recent data suggest that plaintiffs are winning 58 percent of the time and that employers have to pay about $100,000 in each case they lose. Jury awards averaged $250,000 in 1993, and the median award for compensatory damages in 1997 was $250,000. The median punitive damages award was $100,000 that year. . . .

Failure to Avail: Law Versus Reality?

One factor limiting the achievements of *Vinson* and its successors is that much of the burden to resist sexual harassment remains on individual victims to complain and seek redress through their organizations' grievance procedures, press administrative charges, or ultimately file lawsuits. The Supreme Court's twin 1998 employer liability cases, *Faragher* and *Ellerth*, attempted to engineer legal and economic incentives that encourage organizations to take proactive steps to prevent sexual harassment before it occurs or, at least, to remedy it as soon as incidents happen. Roughly stated, employers may have a defense if they provide serviceable policies and procedures against abuse, and victims risk forfeiting their legal remedies unless they reasonably avail themselves of these or alternative means to combat sexual harassment.

The obligation placed on victims to report their harassment contrasts markedly with most victims' responses to sexual harassment. Most sexual harassment targets, as many as 90 to 95 percent, do not report the problem to their employers. Contrary to popular conceptions of men as more assertive and rights conscious, men may be even less likely to take formal action; one survey found that only 7.8 percent of men experiencing same-sex harassment and 3 percent of males claiming harassment by females took formal action. The law and reality appear to be on a collision course.

Reporting Sexual Harassment

Why don't victims report their sexual harassment? Judges, as well as many jurors and the general public, readily perceive this failure as unreasonable, but nonreporting is quite under-standable when viewed from the victim's perspective. Domi-nant ideology may immobilize victims. They may simply not recognize, or name, the behavior as sexual harassment, or they may consider it a personal problem to be solved by individual initiative. Victims may subordinate their interests to those of the organization or minimize the problem to avoid conflict, perhaps interpreting the misconduct as a misunderstanding. They may view their harassment as a minor annoyance or conclude that it is inevitable. About a quarter of all victims blame themselves. Many are ashamed, and others are simply so sickened by the situation that they are unable to make any effective response.

Afraid to Tell

Victims validly fear that they will not be believed. The ideol-ogy of "exit" underestimates the barriers and costs of escaping the situation. Viewing harassment through a lens of "choice" encourages victims to retreat and puts resisters in a double bind: if they report the harassment, they are troublemakers; if they submit, they must have "wanted it." Sensing that the dominant culture still distrusts women's reports of sexual abuse, victims must anticipate that they will be exposing them-selves, as well as their harassers, to skepticism, disbelief, inves-tigation, criticism, ostracism, public humiliation, and further vexation if they have the temerity to blow the whistle on their harassers. Many victims fear the consequences of public accu-sations not only for themselves but also for their loved ones.

Consequences of Reporting

Reporting can entail tangible economic or career conse-quences. Three-quarters of victims have legitimate fears of re-taliation. One study found that 24 percent of victims who complained were fired, and another indicated that a majority of complainants were eventually discharged. Short of termination, victims who complain experience psychological abuse, poorer evaluations and other types of lost benefits, and social ostracism. Beyond discharge, the employer may withhold letters of recommendation, harming prospects for future jobs. Many victims conclude that complaining is tantamount to committing career suicide. Balanced against these grave risks, many victims are likely to perceive few tangible benefits in reporting harassment. Many place little trust in the employer, which, after all, allowed or at least failed to prevent the harassment. And victims may lack faith in the employer's ability or will to remedy the harm of harassment. One survey found that only 20 percent of women believed that complaints were dealt with justly, although 70 percent of personnel managers believed that complaints were resolved appropriately. Organizations sometimes employ a "double discourse" on reporting sexual harassment: although the official policies and procedures discourage harassment and facilitate reporting, a "hidden transcript" of scuttlebutt supplements the official documents, deterring targets from taking formal action.

Responses to Sexual Harassment

Lack of complaint, however, does not mean lack of response. Although studies show that between a quarter and a half of all victims "ignore" the problem, that term may obscure an active decision to try to endure the harassment in the hope that it will dissipate or to temporize while assessing what, if anything, to do about it. Another 25 percent respond "mildly." Such responses may include treating the harassment as a joke, answering with humorous or diversionary retorts, or voicing polite requests to stop the behavior. Many victims simply try to avoid the problem or the harasser. Probably 10 to 20 percent seek a transfer or quit altogether. Few—2 percent, according to one study—seek legal advice, and of those who register charges with the EEOC, only 1 percent follow through with lawsuits.

Nonreporting

Despite these bleak realities, the law and the public generally do not empathize with nonreporting. At trial, the case's circumstances look radically different from when the harassment actually occurred. By trial time, the victim is legally represented and protected, the vague dimensions of the original problem have been clarified, and any penalties for going public have been exacted. Reporting, in other words, appears eminently reasonable, but the victim has already crossed many bridges since the harassment occurred. Then, the conduct likely was ambiguous, and the victim needed to retain her job and perhaps her working relationship with the harasser. Reporting procedures may be unclear, the outcome highly uncertain, and the risks formidable. Temporizing or alternative responses likely appear reasonable, while reporting seems daunting. Although enforcement must rely on complaints, since prevention is not foolproof, to require reporting simultaneously with the initial harassment removes effective hope of relief for most victims.

Liability

Joanna L. Grossman has criticized the new Supreme Court rules on employer liability for shifting the focus in analyzing employer liability from the acts of the employer's agent—that is, the harasser—to the employer's own actions and those of the sexual harassment target. Practically, the *Faragher-Ellerth* rules subvert strict liability and substitute negligence standards. This emphasis could be salutary in stimulating preventive efforts by employers, but it abandons Title VII's goal of compensating victims for its other goal of deterrence. Lower courts, Grossman finds, are interpreting the new rules to give employers a free pass on liability unless their own actions are inadequate. Just as the common law allowed dog owners to escape strict liability until after their dogs had taken a first bite (giving owners notice of the problem), the *Faragher-*

Ellerth rule creates a safe harbor for employers that establish reasonable policies and procedures because the "first bite" of sexual harassment is "free."

The Burdens of Reporting

This stance heightens the centrality of determining what is "reasonable" to expect from sexual harassment victims in terms of availing themselves of avenues of reporting or otherwise resisting harassment. Charitably viewed, the Supreme Court's approach to employer liability is an attempt to structure the legal rules to motivate both employers and victims to be more aggressive in their efforts to eradicate sexual harassment. In the long run, this strategy may prove to be less willfully naive than it appears, judged on past social realities. Although studies document that mandating reporting puts the law at odds with reality, social reality is not static. New employer policies, procedures, and training may make a difference in reporting rates if targets come to believe that they have a right to be free from harassment and that available remedies can realistically stop the harassment. Research in the 1990s suggested that reporting could be expected to increase, and fragmentary evidence supports this hypothesis. A Canadian study found that disseminating antiharassment policies by means ranging from posters to pamphlets to presentations both encouraged women to respond assertively to harassment, including filing complaints, and resulted in fewer incidents of harassment. Jill Kriegsberg suggests practical and philosophical reasons to support a reporting requirement: "Pushing women to report instances of sexual harassment should also be encouraged from a feminist standpoint. It is important for women to be proactive against this problem and by speaking out against such behavior, women send a message that such conduct is not and should not be accepted." Although everyone concerned with eradicating sexual harassment has a stake in changing the reality of nonreporting, it is unclear whether the heavy burdens of reporting can be borne by individual victims absent an organized political response.

Gender Relations and the Courts

In a society that displays a marked penchant for turning political issues into legal disputes, legal clashes often assume epic political proportions. When private plaintiffs such as Mechelle Vinson go to court to protect their interests and to assert their putative rights, they invariably pull courts into broader social controversies. Although ostensibly performing the limited function of applying the law to resolve disputes between individual parties by relying on the conservative technique of following precedent, courts sometimes make decisions that send shock waves of change reverberating throughout society. The story of *Meritor Savings Bank v. Vinson* and its aftermath illustrates how deeply involved the Supreme Court and lower courts have been in the evolution of gender relations, leading to some of the most striking social changes of the late twentieth century. And widely varying assessments of the role played by the law and courts in these and other changes demonstrate how vigorously contested that involvement has been.

> "In effect, the Supreme Court has placed the burden of exposing and eradicating sexual harassment squarely on the shoulders of the victims. By requiring women to come forward and lodge internal complaints, the Court ignored extensive empirical data that overwhelmingly established that women file complaints only as a last resort."

The Hostile Work Environment and Employer Liability for Sexual Harassment

Anna-Maria Marshall

Anna-Maria Marshall has been an associate professor of sociology and law at the University of Illinois College of Law since 1999. Marshall was a litigator from 1985 to 1990 in the areas of employment and labor law. In 2005 she published Confronting Sexual Harassment: The Law and Politics of Everyday Life.

Since the 1970s the courts have handed down a number of decisions defining and clarifying the concept of sexual harassment. In the following selection, Marshall offers a detailed review of several such cases. She stresses that despite progress in the courts, it is the victims in the workplace who still bear the burden of reporting sexual harassment and seeking justice. Furthermore,

Marshall observes that employers are motivated to defend themselves against harassment claims by establishing a formal complaint procedure and taking certain remedial steps after misconduct is reported. Studies have shown that such measures discourage employees from revealing harassment and thus protect the interests of the company, not the victim.

Legal innovation, particularly in the areas of civil rights and civil liberties, emerges from the clash of complex social force. Notably, social movements are often responsible for initially advancing these novel claims that create new legal rights. However, social movements do not exercise complete control over the process or pace of legal innovation, particularly in the judicial arena. Litigation is inherently conflictual, consisting of a dispute between two or more opposing parties. First, the defendants being sued are advancing their own arguments resisting the new rights and legal claims. Of course, judges and juries bring their own perspectives to the conflict and can shape the outcome of the litigation. Out of this mix emerge judicial opinions that give form to the legal rights. Then, once the innovation takes hold and becomes well-established, non-activist lawyers representing paying clients can begin to use it, which may further expand or contract the scope of the right.

Legal Process Shapes Society

These efforts create a legal environment that has the potential to re-shape social relations, although probably never in the way anticipated or even hoped for when social movements begin their law reform efforts. As individuals become informed about their rights, they mobilize them or they may choose to ignore them, both of which can affect the power of the right to constitute social relations. On the other hand, in the face of this new right, the entrenched interests that initially resisted its creation have to adapt. They develop strategies for avoiding liability, and those strategies further shape behavior. This competitive legal environment is filled with specific rules that must be accounted for in any analysis of how law shapes behavior; we need to know what the rules are before we assess the ways that they actually work.

The legal claim for sexual harassment follows this path of legal innovation. Original cases brought by feminist legal activists and civil rights attorneys grounded the claim in equal employment and educational opportunity protected by Title VII (rather than sexual violence, for example). Judicial opinions in the 1970s and 1980s provided definitions of prohibited conduct, beginning with *quid pro quo* harassment [one thing traded for another, such as a job promotion given for sexual favors] and gradually expanding to the hostile working environment. Moreover, the efforts of human resources professionals and employment lawyers and a series of Supreme Court opinions made sexual harassment policies and procedures virtually mandatory in the US workplace....

The Hostile Working Environment

By the late 1970s, women were filing lawsuits with more expansive claims. In these new lawsuits, women described working environments rife with sexual jokes and banter and unwanted physical contact that in some extreme cases constituted sexual assault. Unlike women making claims for *quid pro quo* harassment, however, these women did not lose their jobs or suffer any tangible job-related detriment like loss of a raise or promotion. Nevertheless, they argued, the working environment imposed a substantial burden on their ability to perform their jobs. For example, in 1977, Roxanne Smith filed a complaint for sex discrimination against her employer. In one of the counts of the complaint, she told the court that she had been "subjected to sexual advances and remarks" but conceded that her rejection of these demands not affect any specific working condition (*Smith v. Rust Engineering Company* 1978). The court dismissed this count of the complaint.

Although courts were reluctant to recognize this form of sexual harassment, the EEOC [U.S. Equal Employment Opportunity Commission] had been following the legal issue closely. Catharine MacKinnon and other feminist legal activists consulted with the EEOC to help shape regulations advising employers about how to comply with the growing body of case law. In November 1980, the EEOC issued regulations including conduct such as jokes, threats and demands in its definition of sexual harassment. According to the EEOC, sexual harassment should include "such conduct [that] has the purpose or effect of unreasonably interfering with an individual's work performance or creating an intimidating, hostile or offensive work environment." However, while courts give great deference to the regulations issued by administrative agencies, regulations are merely advisory and do not have the force of law until adopted by a court (*Meritor Savings Bank v. Vinson* 1986).

Key Hostile Environment Cases

The first federal case acknowledging a sex discrimination claim for a hostile working environment was decided in 1981. In *Bundy v. Jackson* (1981), Sandra Bundy described sexual advances made daily by her supervisors and co-workers. For over three years, they constantly asked her out to lunch, invited her to go on vacations, made sexual jokes and even physically molested her by pinching her or caressing her. Once, when she complained about this conduct to a supervisor, he told her he would investigate but then justified his co-workers' actions by observing: "Any man in his right mind would want to rape you." Although the DC Circuit found that Bundy did not suffer any adverse job consequences as a result of her refusal of these offers, the court still held that the hostile working environment itself was sex discrimination. The court asked: "How can sexual harassment, which injects the most demeaning sexual stereotypes into the general work environment and which always represents an intentional assault on an individual's innermost privacy, not be illegal?" Shortly thereafter, the Fourth Circuit acknowledged a claim with similar facts but no physical acts of harassment, thus acknowledging that a hostile working environment could consist of verbal harassment alone (*Katz v. Dole* 1983).

It was not until 1986, when sexual harassment cases had been in the federal courts for almost 15 years, that the Supreme Court issued a decision that put to rest any question that sexual harassment—in *quid pro quo* or hostile working environment situations—constituted sex discrimination in employment. Mechelle Vinson's supervisor at Meritor Savings Bank had made sexual demands on her, including sexually assaulting her in the bank vault. Although her job was never explicitly threatened, Vinson complied with the supervisors's requests because she feared he would fire her. In *Meritor Savings Bank v. Vinson* (1986), the Court endorsed the EEOC's regulations defining a hostile working environment as a workplace where employees faced "unwelcome sexual advances, requests for favors, and other verbal or physical conduct of a sexual nature." The Court continued: "For sexual harassment to be actionable, it must be sufficiently severe or pervasive 'to alter the conditions of [the victim's] employment and create an abusive working environment." Thus, even as it recognized a cause of action for a hostile working environment, the Court placed restrictions on that claim. The plaintiff, it declared, must show that the conduct was unwelcome, which allows the trial to address issues such as the plaintiff's dress and manner. This inquiry can deflect attention away from the harasser's behavior.

In 1993, the Supreme Court further elaborated the definition of a hostile working environment. The Court held that to state a claim for sexual harassment, a plaintiff does not have to demonstrate that she experienced psychological distress (*Harris v. Forklift Systems, Inc.* 1993). On the other hand, to constitute a hostile working environment, the behaviors must also interfere with the employee's performance of her job duties. The Supreme Court in *Harris* observed: "If the victim does not subjectively perceive the environment to be abusive, the conduct has not actually altered the conditions of the victim's employment, and there is no Title VII violation. But Title VII comes into play before the harassing conduct leads to a nervous breakdown."

Definition of Harassment Expanded

The legal definition of sexual harassment has gradually expanded to include more types of conduct. For example, a hostile working environment can now consist of same-sex harassment. Early in the legal history of sexual harassment, perplexed courts pondered how the legal framework would deal with the case of a bisexual supervisor who harassed an employee of the same gender. For example, the trial court in *Corne* [*Corne v. Bausch and Lomb, Inc.*, 1975] observed: "It would be ludicrous to hold that the sort of activity involved here was contemplated by the Act because to do so would mean that if the conduct complained of was directed equally to males there would be no basis for suit." In 1998, the Supreme Court resolved this question by holding that same-sex sexual harassment violated Title VII as long as the plaintiff could prove the statutory requirements: that the harassment was severe and pervasive and that it was discriminatory (*Oncale v. Sundowner Offshore Services, Inc.* 1998). The Court observed:

> In same-sex (as in all) harassment cases, the inquiry requires careful consideration of the social context in which particular behavior occurs and is experienced by its target . . . Common sense, and appropriate sensitivity to social context, will enable courts and juries to distinguish between simple teasing or roughhousing among members of the same sex, and conduct which a reasonable person in the plaintiff's position would find severely hostile or abusive.

The flexibility of the category of sexual harassment is also apparent in the debate surrounding the appropriate legal standard for determining what constitutes an "unreasonable interference" with an employee's working conditions. This debate asks whether judges and juries should evaluate the working environment through the eyes of a reasonable person, a reasonable woman, a reasonable victim, or someone else. Most circuits follow the traditional "reasonable person" standard. The most famous—and most criticized—articulation of this standard came in *Rabidue v. Osceola Refining Company* (1986). Vivienne Rabidue was the only female manager in the company, and one of her co-workers routinely treated her with contempt, using vulgar language to address her. In addition, men posted in their offices pictures and calendars of naked women in demeaning positions. The trial and appellate courts denied that this conduct constituted sexual harassment. Citing the prevalence of near-naked women in magazines and television, the court observed that Rabidue could not have been offended by her co-workers' behavior. The court stated: "The sexually oriented poster displays had a *de minimis* [legally insignificant] effect on the plaintiff's work environment when considered in the context of a society that condones and publicly features and commercially exploits open displays of written and pictorial erotica at the newsstands, on prime-time television, at the cinema, and in other public places."

The "Reasonable Woman" Standard

However, several courts since *Rabidue* have adopted the different "reasonable woman" standard. In the leading case in this area, *Ellison v. Brady* (1991), a woman received notes from a co-worker, asking her out on dates and expressing his hope for a physical relationship with her. Ellison was "shocked" and "frightened" by his notes. In considering whether her harasser's conduct was sufficiently severe, the Ninth Circuit adopted the "reasonable woman" standard, which attempted to account for the different reactions of men and women to sexual attention. The court argued that the reasonable person standard "would run the risk of reinforcing the prevailing level of discrimination." In another case, a female welder working in a shipyard was confronted with pornographic pictures, sexual jokes, and threats every day. The trial court's opinion, documenting every picture, poster, and comment, went on for pages. Admitting that men might not be offended by this environment, the court found that "a reasonable woman would find that the working environment was abusive" (*Robinson v. Jacksonville Shipyards, Inc.*, 1991).

Although the Supreme Court has not yet weighed in on the appropriate standard for evaluating a hostile working environment, it has made some suggestive comments in its most recent sexual harassment cases. For example, in *Harris* the Court used the phrase "reasonable person" while also emphasizing that the plaintiff also had to show subjective harm. According to this ruling, then, the plaintiff has to prove both that she herself was bothered by the behavior and that most people would find the working conditions offensive. Most recently, in *Oncale* the Court stated that the environment "should be judged from the perspective of a reasonable person in the plaintiff's position, considering all the circumstances." Some have suggested that this formulation amounts to a reasonable victim standard, but the Court's cryptic treatment of this issue does little to clear up the confusion since being "in the plaintiff's position" could also include being a woman, thus indirectly importing the reasonable woman standard. Thus, because the Supreme Court has not yet issued a clear statement on the test for reasonableness, the circuit courts of appeal remain divided about the appropriate standard to use in hostile environment cases.

Employer's Liability and Sexual Harassment Policies

An employer's liability for the harassing acts of its supervisors and employees has been a recurring issue in the development of sexual harassment law. Employers have argued that they should not be held responsible for supervisory conduct that they neither authorized nor knew about, and sexual harassment is the paradigmatic example of such conduct. Courts have responded to this argument by holding that employers must adopt grievance procedures that will both protect employees and employers by providing a mechanism for the identification and resolution of problems before they require litigation. In turn, this judicial endorsement of sexual harassment policies has made them proliferate in US work-places.

In its first case on sexual harassment, *Meritor Savings Bank v. Vinson* (1986), the Supreme Court suggested that an appropriately designed policy could protect an employer from sexual harassment. The Court observed:

> If the employer has an expressed policy against sexual harassment and has implemented a procedure specifically designed to resolve sexual harassment claims, and if the victim does not take advantage of that procedure, the employer should be shielded from liability in the absence of actual knowledge of the sexually hostile environment (obtained, e.g., by the filing of a charge with the EEOC or a comparable state agency). In all other cases, the employer will be liable if it has actual knowledge of the harassment or if, considering all the facts of the case, the victim in question had no reasonably available avenue for making his or her complaint known to appropriate management officials.

Although Meritor had a grievance procedure, the Court found that it was unacceptable because it required employees to lodge complaints with their supervisors. The Court noted that such a procedure put employees being harassed by their supervisors in an untenable position and would therefore not protect the employer from being sued.

Elaborating on Employer Liability

During its 1997–1998 term, the Supreme Court elaborated the rules governing an employer's liability for sexual harassment.

In *Faragher v. Boca Raton* (1998), Faragher was a life guard where her supervisors subjected her to sexual comments and unwanted physical contact on a daily basis. Moreover, because they were working at a beach, they were far away from the city's offices and did not come in regular contact with human resources personnel. Although the city had a sexual harassment policy, neither the life guards nor their supervisors were aware of it. Noting that lower courts had been struggling since *Meritor* to come up with manageable standards governing employer's liability, the Supreme Court in *Faragher* and its companion case, *Burlington Industries v. Ellerth* (1998), articulated a new set of standards. First, the Court rejected the argument that employer liability revolved around the distinction between *quid pro quo* and hostile working environment sexual harassment. Instead, under the new rule, courts must ask whether an employee suffered a "direct, negative job consequence." The Court observed that this job consequence could be the result of either form of sexual harassment: the loss of a job benefit from refusing to comply with a sexual demand or a tangible job-related injury resulting from the hostile working environment.

Second, the harasser's authority in the workplace was an important element in the Court's clarified rule on liability. If the harasser was a supervisor, the employer could be held liable for the damage done to the employee, even if the employer did not know about the harassing behaviors. Employers resisted this rule, arguing that the harassing acts were outside the scope of a supervisor's employment duties and did nothing to further the firm's interests. Therefore, employers could not be held responsible for the supervisors' actions. But the Court rejected this position, reasoning:

> When a person with supervisory authority discriminates in the terms and conditions of subordinates' employment, his actions necessarily draw upon his superior position over the people who report to him, or those under them, whereas an

employee generally cannot check a supervisor's abusive conduct the same way that she might deal with abuse from a co-worker. When a fellow employee harasses, the victim can walk away or tell the offender where to go, but it may be difficult to offer such responses to a supervisor, whose "power to supervise—[which may be] to hire and fire, and to set work schedules and pay rates—does not disappear ... when he chooses to harass through insults and offensive gestures rather than directly with threats of firing or promises of promotion." Recognition of employer liability when discriminatory misuse of supervisory authority alters the terms and conditions of a victim's employment is underscored by the fact that the employer has a greater opportunity to guard against misconduct by supervisors than by common workers; employers have greater opportunity and incentive to screen them, train them, and monitor their performance.

Employer Fault Not Automatic

On the other hand, the Court held that when the harasser took no "tangible employment action," employers could not automatically be held liable. Accepting in part the employers' rationale that employees themselves could handle co-worker harassment that did not directly harm them, the Supreme Court endorsed a negligence standard for employer liability and created an affirmative defense for employers seeking to rebut sexual harassment claims:

> When no tangible employment action is taken, a defending employer may raise an affirmative defense to liability or damages, subject to proof by a preponderance of the evidence. The defense comprises two necessary elements: (a) that the employer exercised reasonable care to prevent and correct promptly any sexually harassing behavior, and (b) that the plaintiff employee unreasonably failed to take advantage of any preventive or corrective opportunities provided by the employer or to avoid harm otherwise.

This new standard for liability thus creates new obligations for both employees complaining about sexual harassment and their employers.

Employers Adopt New Policies

Obviously, the new standard articulated in *Faragher* and *Ellerth* required employers to adopt new policies and procedures addressing sexual harassment in the working environment. In fact, the decisions set off a feeding frenzy among human resources professionals and consultants who filled magazines and journals with articles outlining possible policies that would fulfill employers' obligations. Although the Court was vague about the details of such policies, the professionals basically agreed on the bare minimum. First, the policy should define prohibited conduct, provide a list of specific examples, and be widely and regularly distributed to all employees. The procedures should provide multiple avenues for pursuing grievances; employers were advised to designate several managerial positions that could officially receive complaints about sexual harassment. In addition, the policies should not require targets to confront their harassers. Once a complaint has been lodged, managers must investigate by interviewing the parties involved and possible witnesses. Many commentators urge employers to be proactive and pursue these investigations even if the complainant is reluctant to file a formal grievance. Finally, employers were advised to respond promptly to complaints and to take corrective action to redress the problem.

The Supreme Court and human resources literature have suggested that an employer would have to do more than just adopt such policies to establish the affirmative defense that it had "exercised reasonable care" to prevent and redress sexual harassment. Both the courts and human resources experts urged employers to be proactive in monitoring harassment and in responding to complaints promptly and effectively. To demonstrate this proactive concern, some employers now implement training programs in an effort to educate employees about the limits of acceptable work behavior and to teach supervisors about how to handle complaints brought to their attention. In addition to the ameliorative effects on the workplace, such training programs are considered evidence that employers are taking the initiative in preventing sexual harassment, although courts have not yet held that training was (or is) mandatory.

Complaint Procedures Considered

The courts have been notably generous in their interpretation of employers' obligations under the affirmative defense outlined in *Faragher* and *Ellerth*. A study published in 2001 found that in the overwhelming majority of sexual harassment cases following the decisions, employers satisfied this part of the affirmative defense when they showed that they had circulated a sexual harassment policy to their employees and that the policy allowed employees to bypass their harassers in lodging a complaint. In fact, commentators have noted that, under the defense, employers have an interest in designing policies that discourage complaints:

> When a victim complains, the employer, at least theoretically, cannot prevail on the affirmative defense because the second prong requires the plaintiff employee to have unreasonably failed to take advantage of corrective opportunities provided by the employer to avoid harm. Thus, employers may have a disincentive to undertake any employer measures that go beyond the minimum requirements if those additional measures actually *induce* victims to complain.

On the other hand, the new standard imposes an obligation on targets of harassment to complain using the employer's grievance procedure or lose their right to sue. Theoretically, employees have an opportunity to show that they had a good reason for not coming forward, but the study of lower court sexual harassment opinions also showed that no court has accepted any such reason. Every time a plaintiff failed to invoke a grievance procedure, the trial court dismissed the complaint.

Burden Still on Victims

In effect, the Supreme Court has placed the burden of exposing and eradicating sexual harassment squarely on the shoulders of the victims. By requiring women to come forward and lodge internal complaints, the Court ignored extensive empirical data that overwhelmingly established that women file complaints only as a last resort. Moreover, while there is some evidence suggesting that anti-harassment policies, complaint procedures, and training programs have some positive effects, these are not a cure-all for the problem of sexual harassment and may actually distract from finding real solutions.

The legal rules governing sexual harassment have shaped the US workplace in meaningful ways. Most obviously, employers have complied with their legal obligations and adopted grievance policies and procedures that define sexual harassment and provide targets with means for redressing their complaints. Yet by itself, law cannot dictate how these policies actually work. For example, the legal definitions of harassing behaviors remain ambiguous, depending on both objective standards of conduct and a target's subjective experience. Policies will not become relevant, therefore, until a target perceives an experience as sexual harassment. And although the policies theoretically play an important role in employees' ability to vindicate their rights, the procedures are administered by management employees who are chiefly concerned with protecting the employer's interests.

"Today, employee awareness of the right to be free from sexual harassment has grown, and employers are likewise more aware of their duty to take affirmative steps to prevent workplace sexual harassment. Yet it continues to be a significant problem."

The Evolution of Sexual Harassment Law

Debra S. Katz and Avi Kumin

Debra S. Katz is a lawyer and partner at Katz, Marshall & Banks, LLP, in Washington, D.C., and worked on Meritor Savings Bank v. Vinson. *Katz is considered an expert in sexual harassment law. She has appeared on numerous television and radio programs discussing employment law and civil rights issues. Katz has received degrees from Union College and the University of Wisconsin. Avi Kumin is a lawyer and a senior associate at Katz, Marshall & Banks, LLP. He is an employment discrimination and civil rights specialist. Kumin is a member of the District of Columbia and California Bar Associations. He holds degrees from Brandeis University and Yale Law School.*

According to Katz and Kumin, although legal protections against sexual harassment have progressed in the two decades since the landmark Meritor Savings Bank v. Vinson *case, substantial obstacles remain for victims of gender discrimination. The authors maintain that many workers decline to report intimidation for fear of retaliation by their employer, supervisor, or coworkers.*

Debra S. Katz and Avi Kumin, *"Meritor at 20: Ills Persist," National Law Journal,* June 26, 2006. Copyright © 2006 National Law Journal. Reproduced by permission.

*Moreover, Katz and Kumin assert that the law handed down in post-*Meritor *cases requires that alleged harassment be severe or pervasive before legal remedies are available.*

This month [June 2006] marks the 20th anniversary of the U.S. Supreme Court's landmark sexual harassment case, *Meritor Savings Bank v. Vinson*, in which the court held that Title VII of the Civil Rights Act of 1964's bar on discrimination "because of sex" prohibited an employer from subjecting an employee to a sexually hostile work environment. Sexual harassment law has come a long way during this period, although there is still room for improvement.

In *Meritor* Mechelle Vinson came under the supervision of Sydney Taylor, a bank vice president, who repeatedly propositioned her for sex. Vinson reluctantly consented because she thought that she would lose her job if she didn't. Over the next few years, Taylor subjected Vinson to horrific sexual harassment—exposing himself to her at the workplace, fondling her in front of other employees and even raping her on several occasions. When Vinson's Title VII claim reached the Supreme Court, the bank—along with the U.S. Chamber of Commerce and other pro-business *amici curiae*—["friends of the court" who support a party's legal position] argued that Title VII's prohibition of sex discrimination did not encompass "sexual advances towards an individual female employee."

The Supreme Court disagreed. The court had little difficulty in deciding that sexual harassment in the workplace was "because of sex" and therefore illegal under Title VII. Justice William H. Rehnquist, in a unanimous opinion, wrote that Title VII was not limited to only "economic" or "tangible" discrimination, and that "the phrase 'terms, conditions, or privileges of employment' evinces a congressional intent to strike at the entire spectrum of disparate treatment of men and women in employment."

Thomas-Hill Incident Raises Awareness

It took another five years, though, for the term "sexual harassment" to fully enter the public lexicon. In 1991, President George H.W. Bush nominated Clarence Thomas to the Supreme Court. During the Senate confirmation hearings, the press reported that Thomas had been accused of sexual harassment by Anita Hill, a law school professor who had previously worked with him at the Department of Education and the Equal Employment Opportunity Commission (EEOC). While the Senate ultimately confirmed Thomas' appointment by the slimmest of margins, the public learned through the hearings what "sexual harassment" meant and that it was illegal. Following these hearings, the number of employees who filed such claims rose exponentially. (In 1999, the impeachment trial of President Bill Clinton again awakened the public to the intersection of sexual harassment and the law.)

In the 20 years since *Meritor*, sexual harassment law has evolved in several important ways. In 1993, the Supreme Court decided *Harris v. Forklift Systems*, emphasizing that "Title VII comes into play before the harassing conduct leads to a nervous breakdown." In 1998, in *Oncale v. Sundowner Offshore Services*, the court held that "nothing in Title VII necessarily bars a claim of discrimination . . . merely because the plaintiff and the defendant . . . are of the same sex."

Employer Liability Defined

Later that year, the Supreme Court decided two more cases—*Burlington Industries v. Ellerth* and *Faragher v. City of Boca Raton*—which held that an employer is vicariously liable for sexual harassment by its employees, but gave an employer an affirmative defense if it could prove that it exercised reasonable care to prevent and promptly correct the behavior and that the plaintiff unreasonably failed to take advantage of any preventative or corrective opportunities it provided. The court thereby created a large incentive for employers to adopt antiharassment policies, reporting procedures and disciplinary measures aimed at preventing and swiftly responding to workplace sexual harassment.

Today, employee awareness of the right to be free from sexual harassment has grown, and employers are likewise more aware of their duty to take affirmative steps to prevent workplace sexual harassment. Yet it continues to be a significant problem. Last year, nearly 13,000 employees filed charges with the EEOC, and thousands more filed similar complaints with state and local agencies.

When to Report Is Problematic

Although the post-*Meritor* cases have clarified legal issues, real-world cases remain problematic. Out of well-founded fear that a harassing supervisor or co-worker may retaliate if she reports sexual harassment or the hope that the conduct will cease if she simply ignores it, an employee may endure months or years of harassment without remedy. Reinforcing this unfortunate reality is the fact that sexual harassment law emphasizes that the offending behavior must be "sufficiently severe or pervasive" to be actionable. If an employee attempts to quickly forestall sexual harassment by promptly reporting, she may be told—by a human resources department or a court— that it was not sufficiently severe or pervasive. On the other hand, if she waits too long to report, a court may find that the defendant is entitled to the *Faragher/Ellerth* affirmative defense.

The Supreme Court has repeatedly made clear that Title VII should not be transformed into a "general civility code," where every harassing action, no matter how minor, becomes an actionable claim. Yet we should be long past the days when an employee must endure the indignity of working in a sexually hostile work environment or being subjected to unwelcome demands for sex just to be able to earn a paycheck.

CHAPTER 4

Sex Discrimination in Education

Case Overview

Jackson v. Birmingham Board of Education (2005)

Title IX of the Education Amendments of 1972 (Title IX) is a federal statute establishing sex-equality rules and banning sex discrimination in schools and other institutions that receive funding from the federal government. Title IX is perhaps best known for having boosted sports programs for female high-school and college students, which were a mere shadow of male athletes' programs until recent years. In the 2005 case of *Jackson v. Birmingham Board of Education*, the U.S. Supreme Court extended Title IX to protect an individual from retaliation for reporting sex discrimination even when the person was not a direct victim of the original discriminatory acts.

The plaintiff in *Jackson* was a male teacher and coach in the public school system of Birmingham, Alabama. In 1999 he was transferred to a high school where he was assigned to teach physical education and coach the girls' basketball team. He soon discovered that the girls' basketball team did not receive equal funding or access to athletic equipment and facilities compared to the boys' team. He complained of the disparity to his supervisors, but to no avail. At the same time, he began receiving negative work evaluations and ultimately was removed as the girls' coach. He filed suit against the Board of Education, which governed the school system, alleging that the retaliation against him constituted illegal discrimination under Title IX. A federal district court dismissed the teacher's case on the grounds that Title IX did not prohibit retaliation, and the Eleventh Circuit U.S. Court of Appeals agreed.

The U.S. Supreme Court accepted the case for review. The majority opinion in the close 5-4 decision was written by Justice Sandra Day O'Connor, the first-ever female U.S. Supreme

Court justice. The majority broadly interpreted Title IX, emphasizing that Congress created the statute intending to wipe out sex discrimination in the schools and other covered institutions. While retaliation is not explicitly mentioned in Title IX, retaliation for a complaint of sex discrimination is within the statute's intended reach, the majority held. Furthermore, protecting against retaliation would encourage reporting of discrimination and discourage institutions from covering it up, furthering the intent of Congress, O'Connor wrote. Meanwhile, the four dissenting justices pointed out that other anti-discrimination statutes drafted by Congress include specific rules prohibiting retaliation against those who report discriminatory acts. The Court is required to assume that by not including such provisions in Title IX, Congress intended that the statute not cover retaliation, the dissenters contended. They further argued that retaliation against someone for reporting discrimination could not logically be defined as discrimination itself.

As *Jackson* is a relatively recent case, it is unclear how far-reaching the decision will be. Legal commentators have questioned whether courts will broadly interpret the decision, given the close vote by the Supreme Court. Several commentators, like the dissenting justices, have remarked that the majority used strained logic to reach its conclusion. Oddly enough, even some strong supporters of Title IX have taken this view. They are concerned that the alleged logical weakness of the decision will prevent it from being used widely by future victims of retaliation. Some have suggested that a congressional amendment to Title IX specifically protecting against retaliation would be more useful.

"Retaliation is discrimination 'on the basis of sex' because it is an intentional response to the nature of the complaint: an allegation of sex discrimination."

The Court's Decision: Title IX Encompasses Claims of Retaliation Against an Individual Who Complains of Sex Discrimination

Justice Sandra Day O'Connor

Justice Sandra Day O'Connor was appointed to the U.S. Supreme Court in 1981 by President Ronald Reagan. She was the first woman to serve on the Court and remained there until her retirement in 2006. Justice O'Connor was born in El Paso, Texas, in 1930. She graduated magna cum laude from Stanford University in 1950 and received her law degree two years later. Justice O'Connor served in the Arizona State Senate from 1969 to 1975 and was elected Senate majority leader in 1972. She was the assistant attorney general of Arizona from 1965 to 1969.

The following selection is an excerpt from Justice O'Connor's majority opinion in Jackson v. Birmingham Board of Education, *a 2005 case in which the U.S. Supreme Court expanded the reach of Title IX of the Education Amendments of 1972. Title IX established sexual equality rules for schools and other recipients of federal funding, and has helped spur the growth of sports programs for female high school and college students. In*

Justice Sandra Day O'Connor, majority opinion, *Jackson v. Birmingham Board of Education*, 544 U.S. 167, 2005.

the case of Jackson v. Birmingham Board of Education, *the Court ruled that a male teacher who faced retaliation after complaining about discrimination against females in a high school's athletic program could pursue legal action against the school district under Title IX. The Court held that Title IX protects individuals against retaliation relating to gender bias, even if the victim of the retribution was not the subject of the original inequity.*

Title IX [of the Education Amendments of 1972] prohibits sex discrimination by recipients of federal education funding. The statute provides that "[n]o person in the United States shall, on the basis of sex, be excluded from participation in, be denied the benefits of, or be subjected to discrimination under any education program or activity receiving Federal financial assistance." [Citations omitted throughout.] More than 25 years ago, in *Cannon v. University of Chicago,* (1979), we held that Title IX implies a private right of action to enforce its prohibition on intentional sex discrimination. In subsequent cases, we have defined the contours of that right of action. In *Franklin v. Gwinnett County Public Schools* we held that it authorizes private parties to seek monetary damages for intentional violations of Title IX. We have also held that the private right of action encompasses intentional sex discrimination in the form of a recipient's deliberate indifference to a teacher's sexual harassment of a student, *Gebser v. Lago Vista Independent School Dist.,* (1998), or to sexual harassment of a student by another student, *Davis v. Monroe County Bd. of Ed.* (1999).

In all of these cases, we relied on the text of Title IX, which, subject to a list of narrow exceptions not at issue here, broadly prohibits a funding recipient from subjecting any person to "discrimination" "on the basis of sex." Retaliation against a person because that person has complained of sex discrimination is another form of intentional sex discrimination encompassed by Title IX's private cause of action. Retaliation is, by definition, an intentional act. It is a form of "discrimination" because the complainant is being subjected to differential treatment. Moreover retaliation is discrimination "on the basis of sex" because it is an intentional response to the nature of the complaint: an allegation of sex discrimination. We conclude that when a funding recipient retaliates against a person *because* he complains of sex discrimination, this constitutes intentional "discrimination" "on the basis of sex," in violation of Title IX.

Law Protects Against Retaliation

The Court of Appeals' conclusion that Title IX does not prohibit retaliation because the "statute makes no mention of retaliation," ignores the import of our repeated holdings construing "discrimination" under Title IX broadly. Though the statute does not mention sexual harassment, we have held that sexual harassment is intentional discrimination encompassed by Title IX's private right of action. Thus, a recipient's deliberate indifference to a teacher's sexual harassment of a student also "violate[s] Title IX's plain terms" [quoting the *Davis* case, above]. Likewise, a recipient's deliberate indifference to sexual harassment of a student by another student also squarely constitutes "discrimination" "on the basis of sex." "Discrimination" is a term that covers a wide range of intentional unequal treatment; by using such a broad term, Congress gave the statute a broad reach.

Congress certainly could have mentioned retaliation in Title IX expressly, as it did in § 704 of Title VII of the Civil Rights Act of 1964. Title VII, however, is a vastly different statute from Title IX, and the comparison the Board urges us to draw is therefore of limited use. Title IX's cause of action is implied, while Title VII's is express. Title IX is a broadly written general prohibition on discrimination, followed by specific, narrow exceptions to that broad prohibition. By contrast, Title VII spells out in greater detail the conduct that constitutes discrimination in violation of that statute. Because Congress did not list *any* specific discriminatory practices when it wrote Title IX, its failure to mention one such practice does not tell us anything about whether it intended that practice to be covered.

Past Anti-Retaliation Rulings

Title IX was enacted in 1972, three years after our decision in *Sullivan v. Little Hunting Park, Inc.* In *Sullivan*, we held that Rev. Stat. § 1978, 42 U. S. C. § 1982, which provides that "[a]ll citizens of the United States shall have the same right . . . as is enjoyed by white citizens . . . to inherit, purchase, lease, sell, hold, and convey real and personal property," protected a white man who spoke out against discrimination toward one of his tenants and who suffered retaliation as a result. Sullivan had rented a house to a black man and assigned him a membership share and use rights in a private park. The corporation that owned the park would not approve the assignment to the black lessee. Sullivan protested, and the corporation retaliated against him by expelling him and taking his shares. Sullivan sued the corporation, and we upheld Sullivan's cause of action under 42 U. S. C. § 1982 for "[retaliation] for the advocacy of [the black person's] cause." Thus, in *Sullivan* we interpreted a general prohibition on racial discrimination to cover retaliation against those who advocate the rights of groups protected by that prohibition.

Congress enacted Title IX just three years after *Sullivan* was decided, and accordingly that decision provides a valuable context for understanding the statute. As we recognized in *Cannon,* "it is not only appropriate but also realistic to presume that Congress was thoroughly familiar with *[Sullivan]* and that it expected its enactment [of Title IX] to be interpreted in conformity with [it]." Retaliation for Jackson's advocacy of the rights of the girls' basketball team in this case is "discrimination" "on the basis of sex," just as retaliation for advocacy on behalf of a black lessee in *Sullivan* was discrimination on the basis of race.

Board's Arguments Rejected

The Board contends that our decision in *Alexander v. Sandoval* (2001), compels a holding that Title IX's private right of action does not encompass retaliation. *Sandoval* involved an interpretation of Title VI of the Civil Rights Act of 1964, which provides in §601 that no person shall, "on the ground of race, color, or national origin, be excluded from participation in, be denied the benefits of, or be subjected to discrimination under any program or activity" covered by Title VI. Section 602 of Title VI authorizes federal agencies to effectuate the provisions in §601 by enacting regulations. Pursuant to that authority, the Department of Justice promulgated regulations forbidding funding recipients from adopting policies that had "the effect of subjecting individuals to discrimination because of their race, color, or national origin." The *Sandoval* petitioners brought suit to enjoin an English-only policy of the Alabama Department of Public Safety on grounds that it disparately impacted non-English speakers in violation of the regulations. Though we assumed that the regulations themselves were valid, we rejected the contention that the private right of action to enforce intentional violations of Title VI encompassed suits to enforce the disparate-impact regulations. We did so because "[i]t is clear . . . that the disparate-impact regulations do not simply apply to §601—since they indeed forbid conduct that §601 permits—and therefore clear that the private right of action to enforce §601 does not include a private right to enforce these regulations." Thus, *Sandoval* held that private parties may not invoke Title VI regulations to obtain redress for disparate-impact discrimination because Title VI itself prohibits only intentional discrimination.

The Board cites a Department of Education regulation prohibiting retaliation "against any individual for the purpose of interfering with any right or privilege secured by [Title IX]," and contends that Jackson, like the petitioners in *Sandoval*, seeks an "impermissible extension of the statute" when he argues that Title IX's private right of action encompasses retaliation. This argument, however, entirely misses the point. We do not rely on regulations extending Title IX's protection beyond its statutory limits; indeed, we do not rely on the Department of Education's regulation at all, because the statute *itself* contains the necessary prohibition. As we explain above, the text of Title IX prohibits a funding recipient from retaliating against a person who speaks out against sex discrimination, because such retaliation is intentional "discrimination" "on the basis of sex." We reach this result based on the statute's text. In step with *Sandoval*, we hold that Title IX's private right of action encompasses suits for retaliation, because retaliation falls within the statute's prohibition of intentional discrimination on the basis of sex.

Nor are we convinced by the Board's argument that, even if Title IX's private right of action encompasses discrimination, Jackson is not entitled to invoke it because he is an "indirect victi[m]" of sex discrimination. The statute is broadly worded; it does not require that the victim of the retaliation must also be the victim of the discrimination that is the subject of the original complaint. If the statute provided instead that "no person shall be subjected to discrimination on the basis of *such individual's* sex," then we would agree with the Board. However, Title IX contains no such limitation. Where the retaliation occurs because the complainant speaks out about sex discrimination, the "on the basis of sex" requirement is satisfied. The complainant is himself a victim of discriminatory retaliation, regardless of whether he was the subject of the original complaint. As we explain above, this is consistent with *Sullivan*, which formed an important part of the backdrop against which Congress enacted Title IX. *Sullivan* made clear that retaliation claims extend to those who oppose discrimination against others.

Encourages Reporting of Discrimination

Congress enacted Title IX not only to prevent the use of federal dollars to support discriminatory practices, but also "to provide individual citizens effective protection against those practices." We agree with the United States [which filed a supporting brief in the case] that this objective "would be difficult, if not impossible, to achieve if persons who complain about sex discrimination did not have effective protection against retaliation." If recipients were permitted to retaliate freely, individuals who witness discrimination would be loathe to report it, and all manner of Title IX violations might go unremedied as a result.

Reporting incidents of discrimination is integral to Title IX enforcement and would be discouraged if retaliation against those who report went unpunished. Indeed, if retaliation were not prohibited, Title IX's enforcement scheme would unravel. Recall that Congress intended Title IX's private right of action to encompass claims of a recipient's deliberate indifference to sexual harassment. Accordingly, if a principal sexually harasses a student, and a teacher complains to the school board but the school board is indifferent, the board would likely be liable for a Title IX violation. But if Title IX's private right of action does not encompass retaliation claims, the teacher would have no recourse if he were subsequently fired for speaking out. Without protection from retaliation, individuals who witness discrimination would likely not report it, indifference claims would be short-circuited, and the underlying discrimination would go unremedied.

Title IX's enforcement scheme also depends on individual reporting because individuals and agencies may not bring suit under the statute unless the recipient has received "actual notice" of the discrimination. If recipients were able to avoid such notice by retaliating against all those who dare complain, the statute's enforcement scheme would be subverted. We should not assume that Congress left such a gap in its scheme.

Moreover, teachers and coaches such as Jackson are often in the best position to vindicate the rights of their students because they are better able to identify discrimination and bring it to the attention of administrators. Indeed, sometimes adult employees are "the only effective adversar[ies]" of discrimination in schools.

Institutions Aware of Liability

The Board is correct in pointing out that, because Title IX was enacted as an exercise of Congress' powers under the Spending Clause, "private damages actions are available only where recipients of federal funding had adequate notice that they could be liable for the conduct at issue [quoting the *Davis* case]." When Congress enacts legislation under its spending power, that legislation is "in the nature of a contract: in return for federal funds, the States agree to comply with federally imposed conditions." As we have recognized, "[t]here can ... be no knowing acceptance [of the terms of the contract] if a State is unaware of the conditions [imposed by the legislation on its receipt of funds]."

The Board insists that we should not interpret Title IX to prohibit retaliation because it was not on notice that it could be held liable for retaliating against those who complain of Title IX violations. We disagree. Funding recipients have been on notice that they could be subjected to private suits for intentional sex discrimination under Title IX since 1979, when we decided *Cannon*. [Despite the Board's argument, *Pennhurst*, a more recent case] does not preclude private suits for intentional acts that clearly violate Title IX.

Indeed, in *Davis*, we held that *Pennhurst* did not pose an obstacle to private suits for damages in cases of a recipient's deliberate indifference to one student's sexual harassment of another, because the deliberate indifference constituted intentional discrimination on the basis of sex. Similarly, we held in *Gebser* that a recipient of federal funding could be held liable for damages under Title XI for deliberate indifference to a teacher's harassment of a student. In *Gebser*, as in *Davis*, we acknowledge that federal funding recipients must have notice that they will be held liable for damages. But we emphasized that "this limitation on private damages actions is not a bar to liability where a funding recipient intentionally violates the statute." Simply put, "*Pennhurst* does not bar a private damages action under Title IX where the funding recipient engages in intentional conduct that violates the clear terms of the statute."

Retaliation as Cover-Up Prohibited

Thus, the Board should have been put on notice by the fact that our cases since *Cannon*, such as *Gebser* and *Davis* have consistently interpreted Title IX's private cause of action broadly to encompass diverse forms of intentional sex discrimination. Indeed, retaliation presents an even easier case than deliberate indifference. It is easily attributable to the funding recipient, and it is always—by definition—intentional. We therefore conclude that retaliation against individuals because they complain of sex discrimination is "intentional conduct that violates the clear terms of the statute," and that Title IX itself therefore supplied sufficient notice to the Board that it could not retaliate against Jackson after he complained of discrimination against the girls' basketball team.

The regulations implementing Title IX clearly prohibit retaliation and have been on the books for nearly 30 years. More importantly, the Courts of Appeals that had considered the question at the time of the conduct at issue in this case all had already interpreted Title IX to cover retaliation. The Board could not have realistically supposed that, given this context, it remained free to retaliate against those who reported sex discrimination. A reasonable school board would realize that institutions covered by Title IX cannot cover up violations of that law by means of discriminatory retaliation.

To prevail on the merits, Jackson will have to prove that the Board retaliated against him *because* he complained of sex discrimination. The amended complaint alleges that the Board retaliated against Jackson for complaining to his supervisor, Ms. Evelyn Baugh, about sex discrimination at Ensley High School. At this stage of the proceedings, "[t]he issue is not whether a plaintiff will ultimately prevail but whether the claimant is entitled to offer evidence to support the claims." Accordingly, the judgment of the Court of Appeals for the Eleventh Circuit is reversed, and the case is remanded for further proceedings consistent with this opinion.

It is so ordered.

"Under the majority's reasoning, courts may expand liability as they, rather than Congress, see fit. This is no idle worry. The next step is to say that someone closely associated with the complainer, who claims he suffered retaliation for those complaints, likewise has a retaliation claim under Title IX."

Dissenting Opinion: Title IX Does Not Prohibit Retaliation

Justice Clarence Thomas

Justice Clarence Thomas has served on the U.S. Supreme Court since his appointment in 1991 by President George H. W. Bush. Justice Thomas was born near Savannah, Georgia, in 1948. He has degrees from Holy Cross College and Yale Law School. From 1974 to 1977, Justice Thomas was the assistant attorney general of Missouri. Before serving on the Supreme Court, he worked for the U.S. Court of Appeals for the District of Columbia Circuit, U.S. Equal Employment Opportunity Commission, and U.S. Department of Education.

The following excerpt is from the dissent written by Justice Thomas in Jackson v. Birmingham Board of Education, *the 2005 case in which the U.S. Supreme Court extended the reach of Title IX to cover retaliation against those who report instances of sexual discrimination. Here, Thomas argues that the language and history of Title IX do not support the protection of individuals who are not the direct victims of gender inequity.*

Justice Clarence Thomas, dissenting opinion, *Jackson v. Birmingham Board of Education*, 544 U.S. 167, 2005.

The Court holds that the private right of action under Title IX of the Education Amendments of 1972, for sex discrimination that it implied in *Cannon v. University of Chicago*, extends to claims of retaliation. Its holding is contrary to the plain terms of Title IX, because retaliatory conduct is not discrimination on the basis of sex. Moreover, we require Congress to speak unambiguously in imposing conditions on funding recipients through its spending power. And, in cases in which a party asserts that a cause of action should be implied, we require that the statute itself evince a plain intent to provide such a cause of action. Section 901 of Title IX meets none of these requirements. I therefore respectfully dissent.

Title IX provides education funding to States, subject to §901's condition that "[n]o person in the United States shall, on the basis of sex, be excluded from participation in, be denied the benefits of, or be subjected to discrimination under any education program or activity receiving Federal financial assistance." Section 901 does not refer to retaliation. Consequently, the statute prohibits such conduct only if it falls within §901's prohibition against discrimination "on the basis of sex." It does not.

Statue Does Not Cover Retaliation

A claim of retaliation is not a claim of discrimination on the basis of sex. In the context of §901, the natural meaning of the phrase "on the basis of sex" is on the basis of the plaintiff's sex, not the sex of some other person. For example, suppose a sexist air traffic controller withheld landing permission for a plane because the pilot was a woman. While the sex discrimination against the female pilot no doubt adversely impacted male passengers aboard that plane, one would never say that they were discriminated against "on the basis of sex" by the controller's action.

Congress' usage of the phrase "on the basis of sex" confirms this commonsense conclusion. Even within Title VII of the Civil Rights Act of 1964 itself, Congress used the phrase "on the basis of sex" as a shorthand for discrimination "on the basis of such individual's sex." Specifically, in ensuring that Title VII reached discrimination because of pregnancy, Congress provided that "[t]he terms 'because of sex' or 'on the basis of sex' include, but are not limited to, because of or on the basis of pregnancy, childbirth or related medical conditions." The reference to "on the basis of sex" in this provision must refer to Title VII's prohibition on discrimination "because of such individual's . . . sex," suggesting that Congress used the phrases interchangeably. After all, Title VII's general prohibition against discriminatory employer practices does not use "[t]he terms 'because of sex' or 'on the basis of sex.'" It uses only the phrase "because of such individual's . . . sex."

This Court has also consistently used the phrase "on the basis of sex" as a shorthand for on the basis of the claimant's sex. Thus, for a disparate-treatment claim to be a claim of discrimination on the basis of sex, the claimant's sex must have "actually played a role in [the decision-making] process and had a determinative influence on the outcome," *Hazen Paper Co. v. Biggins*, (1993).

Only Victim's Gender Relevant

Jackson's assertion that the Birmingham Board of Education (Board) retaliated against him fails to allege sex discrimination in this sense. Jackson does not claim that his own sex played any role, let alone a decisive or predominant one, in the decision to relieve him of his position. Instead, he avers that he complained to his supervisor about sex discrimination against the girls' basketball team and that, sometime subsequent to his complaints, he lost his coaching position. At best, then, he alleges discrimination "on the basis of sex" founded on the attenuated connection between the supposed adverse treatment and the sex of others. Because Jackson's claim for-retaliation is not a claim that his sex played a role in his adverse treatment, the statute's plain terms do not encompass it.

Jackson's lawsuit therefore differs fundamentally from other examples of sex discrimination, like sexual harassment. A victim of sexual harassment suffers discrimination because of her own sex, not someone else's. Cases in which this Court has held that §901 reaches claims of vicarious liability for sexual harassment are therefore inapposite here. In fact, virtually every case in which this Court has addressed Title IX concerned a claimant who sought to recover for discrimination because of her own sex. Again, Jackson makes no such claim.

Link to Sex Discrimination Weak

Moreover, Jackson's retaliation claim lacks the connection to actual sex discrimination that the statute requires. Jackson claims that he suffered reprisal because he *complained about* sex discrimination, not that the sex discrimination underlying his complaint occurred. This feature of Jackson's complaint is not surprising, since a retaliation claimant need not prove that the complained-of sex discrimination happened. Although this Court has never addressed the question, no Court of Appeals requires a complainant to show more than that he had a reasonable, good-faith belief that discrimination occurred to prevail on a retaliation claim. Retaliation therefore cannot be said to be discrimination on the basis of anyone's sex, because a retaliation claim may succeed where no sex discrimination ever took place.

The majority ignores these fundamental characteristics of retaliation claims. Its sole justification for holding that Jackson has suffered sex discrimination is its statement that "retaliation is discrimination 'on the basis of sex' because it is an intentional response to the nature of the complaint: an allegation of sex discrimination." But the sex-based topic of the complaint cannot overcome the fact that the retaliation is not based on anyone's sex, much less the complainer's sex. For ex-

171

ample, if a coach complains to school officials about the dismantling of the men's swimming team, which he honestly and reasonably, but incorrectly, believes is occurring because of the sex of the team, and he is fired, he may prevail. Yet, he would not have been discriminated against on the basis of his sex, for his own sex played no role, and the men's swimming team over which he expressed concern also suffered no discrimination on the basis of sex. In short, no discrimination on the basis of sex has occurred.

Retaliation Is a Separate Issue

At bottom, and petitioner as much as concedes, retaliation is a claim that aids in enforcing another separate and distinct right. In other contexts, this Court has recognized that protection from retaliation is separate from direct protection of the primary right and serves as a prophylactic measure to guard the primary right. As we explained with regard to Title VII's retaliation prohibition, "a primary purpose of antiretaliation provisions" is "[m]aintaining unfettered access to statutory remedial mechanisms." To describe retaliation as discrimination on the basis of sex is to conflate the enforcement mechanism with the right itself, something for which the statute's text provides no warrant.

Moreover, that the text of Title IX does not mention retaliation is significant. By contrast to Title IX, Congress enacted a separate provision in Title VII to address retaliation, in addition to its general prohibition on discrimination. Congress' failure to include similar text in Title IX shows that it did not authorize private retaliation actions. This difference cannot be dismissed, as the majority suggests, on the ground that Title VII is a more specific statute in which Congress proscribed particular practices, as opposed to the general prohibition here. The fact that Congress created those specific prohibitions in Title VII is evidence that it intended to preclude courts from implying similar specific prohibitions in Title IX.

Even apart from Title VII, Congress expressly prohibited retaliation in other discrimination statutes. If a prohibition on "discrimination" plainly encompasses retaliation, the explicit reference to it in these statutes, as well as in Title VII, would be superfluous—a result we eschew in statutory interpretation. The better explanation is that when Congress intends to include a prohibition against retaliation in a statute, it does so. Its failure to do so in §901 is therefore telling. . . .

Court's Ruling Unsupported

The Court establishes a prophylactic enforcement mechanism designed to encourage whistleblowing about sex discrimination. The language of Title IX does not support this holding. The majority also offers nothing to demonstrate that its prophylactic rule is necessary to effectuate the statutory scheme. Nothing prevents students—or their parents—from complaining about inequality in facilities or treatment. Under the majority's reasoning, courts may expand liability as they, rather than Congress, see fit. This is no idle worry. The next step is to say that someone closely associated with the complainer, who claims he suffered retaliation for those complaints, likewise has a retaliation claim under Title IX.

By crafting its own additional enforcement mechanism, the majority returns this Court to the days in which it created remedies out of whole cloth to effectuate its vision of congressional purpose. In doing so, the majority substitutes its policy judgments for the bargains struck by Congress, as reflected in the statute's text. The question before us is only whether Title IX prohibits retaliation, not whether prohibiting it is good policy. For the reasons addressed above, I would hold that §901 does not encompass private actions for retaliation. I respectfully dissent.

"This Supreme Court decision is a wake-up call. While laws are in place to guarantee rights, they are useless if parents, coaches and athletes don't stand up for their rights."

Stand Up for Title IX Protection

Alison Sawyer

Alison Sawyer is a public relations consultant for the Women's Sports Foundation. Professional athlete Billie Jean King founded the Women's Sports Foundation, an educational organization devoted to female participation in sports and physical activity, in 1974. The Women's Sports Foundation is supported through charitable contributions and is located in Nassau County, New York.

In the following selection Sawyer presents the viewpoints of women athletes, coaches, and celebrities who encourage the reporting of sexual discrimination in order to ensure that Title IX protections are not weakened by complacency and politics. She encourages parents, coaches, and teachers to defend the rights of female athletes under Title IX.

On March 29, 2005, the U.S. Supreme Court ruled on the *Jackson v. Birmingham* case in which a male coach who was fired because he tried to get the same facilities and treatment for the girls he coached that the boys had long enjoyed was told by a lower court that he couldn't sue as a whistle-blower because the word "retaliation" didn't appear in the Title IX statute. In its decision, Justice Sandra Day O'Connor wrote for the majority, "Retaliation against a person because that person has complained of sex discrimination is another form of intentional sex discrimination." She acknowledged that coaches such as Jackson are often in the best position to vindicate the rights of their students because they can see bias and bring it to the attention of administrators. O'Connor said that even though Congress did not explicitly cover retaliation in Title IX, it sought expansive prohibition against sex bias.

Women's Sports Foundation CEO Donna Lopiano called upon parents, coaches, teachers and athletes to document their Title IX discrimination concerns in writing. "Each year, the Women's Sports Foundation's 800 number receives hundreds of calls from distressed parents who are afraid to raise Title IX concerns because they fear retaliation against their athlete daughters—loss of scholarship assistance, being benched and/or harassment by boys' teams whose coaches tell them that because the girls are raising equal treatment issues they will lose financial support or current benefits. They don't want their children to suffer, but they want gender equity laws enforced. Similarly, like Coach Jackson in this Supreme Court case, coaches and teachers who want to raise Title IX issues are afraid they are going to lose their jobs or promotions, get poor performance evaluations or be shunned by colleagues coaching male teams. Coaches whisper on the phone because they are calling from their offices and fear being overheard. Even college alumni suffer retaliation. There are colleges who disband established alumni advisory councils when they raise Title IX issues. These people who care about their daughters and students want to know if someone else can bring concerns forward. This decision is important because it directly addresses this climate of fear."

Testimonials from Athletes and Others

Geena Davis, a Foundation trustee, is a strong Title IX advocate who established www.GeenaTakesAim.com to educate parents and female athletes about their rights under Title IX, stated, "One of the most important steps to take is to document Title IX concerns. How are female athletes being treated unfairly? These concerns must be put in writing and sent to school leaders and even the media. It's too easy for schools to practice subtle and overt retaliation that intimidates parents or students into silence or say they will look into the matter and stall until those who raise issues graduate." Nancy Hogshead-Makar, a former president of the Women's Sports Foundation, professor at the Florida Coastal School of Law, Olympic champion and author of the Women's Sports Foundation's *amicus* ["friend of the court"] brief in the case, said "While I am proud to have played a small part in this significant win, I'm more hopeful now that this decision will empower coaches to be terrific advocates for young girls and women and fulfill the promise of Title IX; true gender-equity in athletics. Coach Jackson's situation is anything but an isolated occurrence; we are facing a rampant problem. This Supreme Court decision was needed to support the voices of those who would stand up for our daughters."

"This Supreme Court decision is a wake-up call. While laws are in place to guarantee rights, they are useless if parents, coaches and athletes don't stand up for their rights," said Women's Sports Foundation President Dominique Dawes.

The Office for Civil Rights of the Department of Education has not initiated a Title IX athletics investigation on its own since 2002. The Department of Education has consistently attempted to weaken Title IX protection, first with a 2003 commission report calling for lower standards that was soundly defeated in the court of public opinion and withdrawn. Now, just last week [March 2005], the Department issued a so-called letter of clarification that created a giant Title

IX loophole, a significant change in policy, allowing institutions to evade equal participation requirements by simply administering an e-mail survey to demonstrate females aren't interested in playing sports.

Dawes continued, "While the Supreme Court decision is welcome, let us recognize that Title IX is under attack by the federal agency charged with its enforcement."

"Jackson v. Birmingham Board of Education (Jackson III) *makes it clear that retaliation claims are now actionable under Title IX.*"

The Pursuit of Gender Equity Under Title IX

Sue Ann Mota

Sue Ann Mota, a professor in legal studies at Bowling Green State University, has served several terms as chair of the Intercollegiate Athletics Committee. She holds a law degree from the University of Toledo, and both an MA and BA from Bowling Green State University.

In the following selection Mota studies the Jackson *case in terms of its impact on the enforcement of Title IX, predicting that many additional retaliation claims will be filed against federally funded schools by alleged victims of sex discrimination. She emphasizes Justice Sandra Day O'Connor's role in upholding women's rights during her tenure on the Court, and ponders how the* Jackson *decision may have differed if the case were argued after Justice O'Connor's retirement in 2006. While she applauds the Court's decision, she admits that she would have preferred that Congress revise the Title IX law to explicitly prohibit retaliatory measures.*

Sue Ann Mota, "Articles: Title IX After Thirty-Four Years—Retaliation Is Not Allowed According to the Supreme Court in *Jackson v. Birmingham Board of Education,*" *Villanova Sports & Entertainment Law Journal*, vol. 13, 2006, pp. 245–70, 266–70. © 2006 Villanova University. Reproduced by permission.

In 1972, Congress enacted Title IX [of the Education Amendments of 1972] to ensure that no person in the U.S. would be excluded from, denied the benefits of, or subjected to discrimination by any educational institution receiving federal funds on the basis of sex. In its thirty-four year history, Title IX has been the subject of an implementing regulation; a policy interpretation, including a three-prong test; a clarification of the three-prong test; a further clarification of that test; and most recently, additional clarification of the three-prong test and a guide to developing student interest surveys under Title IX. Title IX has also been the subject of extensive litigation, including Supreme Count decisions in *Cannon v. University of Chicago* [(1979) private lawsuit that was maintained under Title IX, though not specifically authorized by the statute], *North Haven Board of Education v. Bell* [(1982) court upheld the validity of certain Title IX regulations], *Grove City College v. Bell* [(1984) narrowly interpreted certain Title IX language and effectively removed athletic departments from Title IX coverage—later overturned by future legislation], *Franklin v. Gwinnett County Public Schools* [(1992) see reference below], *Gebser v. Lago Vista Independent School District* [(1998) see reference below], *Davis v. Monroe County Board of Education* [(1999) see reference below], and most recently in *Jackson v. Birmingham Board of Education (Jackson III)* [(2005) allowed lawsuit under Title IX by a victim of retaliation for reporting sexual discrimination, even when the victim of retaliation was not subjected to the sex discrimination]. Title IX has additionally been the subject of numerous other circuit court decisions. . . .

Moreover, Title IX has sparked numerous debates and strong feelings on both sides. Some estimate that more than 350 men's athletic programs have been eliminated in response, at least in part, to Title IX's demands. Others, however, opine that, "while impressive strides have been made for female students since Title IX's inception thirty years ago, females are still imbued with the attitude that athletic employment, participation opportunities, and benefits are a gift and not an entitlement."

The Supreme Court's Interpretations of Title IX

Title IX and its regulations have played an important role in providing opportunities and preventing discrimination on the basis of sex to those who participate in and receive benefits from federally funded institutions. Coaches, administrators, and student athletes must be aware of Title IX's complex regulatory environment and judicial interpretations. The U.S. Supreme Court has interpreted Title IX on numerous occasions. In March, 2005, the U.S. Supreme Court most recently held that Title IX's implied private right of action now also includes retaliation because an individual has raised concerns about sex discrimination. This landmark ruling now explicitly puts educational institutions receiving federal funds on notice that retaliating against an individual who complains about sex discrimination will not be allowed under Title IX. Thus, school boards and school districts should immediately amend policies, procedures, and Title IX enforcement to reflect this landmark Supreme Court decision in order to prevent retaliation against individuals who complain about sex discrimination. If an institution wishes to make an adverse decision against an individual who has previously complained of sex discrimination, the institution must ensure that the decision was nonretaliatory in nature, clearly documented, and legally defensible.

Retaliation

Retaliation is already prohibited in several federal employee protection statutes. Title VII of the Civil Rights Act of 1964, the Age Discrimination in Employment Act, the Americans with Disabilities Act, and the Equal Pay Act all statutorily prohibit an employer's retaliation. The essential elements of a retaliation claim are 1) the employee engaged in a protected activity, 2) there was an adverse action by the employer, and 3) there is a causal connection between the protected activity and the adverse action. In the 2004 fiscal year, the EEOC received 22,740 charges of retaliation discrimination based upon all statutes enforced by the EEOC. In 2004, discharge was alleged in 66 percent of the suits filed by the EEOC with retaliation as a basis of the suit. The likely impact of *Jackson III* will be that more retaliation claims and suits will be filed by those alleging discrimination on the basis of sex in federally funded educational institutions.

Protection for Whistleblowers

The removal of sex discrimination from educational institutions which receive federal funds and the prohibition of retaliation against whistleblowers at such institutions are strongly supported. While this author concurs in the outcome of *Jackson III*, this author would be more comfortable with the prohibition coming from Congress instead of the courts. For example, Congress has expanded whistleblower protection under the Sarbanes-Oxley Act, which provides that publicly traded firms may not retaliate against their whistle-blowing employees. Sarbanes-Oxley also explicitly criminalizes intentional retaliation, including the interference with lawful employment, against whistleblowers. Perhaps if the *Jackson III* decision had swung five-to-four in the other direction, Congress would have remedied this omission as they did with the Civil Rights Restoration Act after the *Grove City College* case. As the *Jackson III* dissent states, this is not a statement about the merits of an anti-retaliation policy, but it is rather a statement that notice to the educational institutions affected must be *clear and unambiguous* under the Spending Clause. Instead, an anti-retaliation, pro-whistleblower policy would have been preferable.

Justice O'Connor's Role

Justice Sandra Day O'Connor, the first woman to serve on the U.S. Supreme Court, played a key role in upholding rights under Title IX. Justice O'Connor authored the majority opinion in *Jackson III*. While Justice O'Connor concurred with the majority in the narrow holding in *Grove City College v. Bell*, Justice O'Connor joined the majority in *Franklin v. Gwinnett County Public Schools*, holding that damages are available under Title IX. Justice O'Connor authored the majority opinion in *Gebser*, which held that a school district is not liable in damages for sexual harassment by a teacher, unless there was actual notice of and indifference to the teacher's conduct. A year later in *Davis v. Monroe County Board of Education*, however, Justice O'Connor authored the majority decision holding that student-on-student sexual harassment is actionable if the board acted with deliberate indifference and the harassment was sufficiently severe, pervasive, and offensive. The *Davis* majority consisted of Justices O'Connor, Stevens, Souter, Ginsburg, and Breyer; while the more conservative Justices Scalia and Thomas, along with Kennedy and the Chief Justice Rehnquist, dissented. By authoring numerous of these opinions, Justice O'Connor has thus left her mark on Title IX jurisprudence.

Justice Alito's Views

At the time of this publication, Justice O'Connor has retired from the Court and Judge Samuel Alito has been confirmed. It is interesting to speculate that had *Jackson III* come to the Court one year later, it may have swung five-to-four the other way, leaving it to Congress to add retaliation to the Title IX statute, as other federal employee protection statutes provide. Judge Alito, while serving on the Third Circuit Court of Appeals, authored an opinion in *Robinson v. City of Pittsburgh*, which held that allegedly retaliatory conduct on the part of the employer did not give rise to a claim of retaliation. While

Robinson's complaint with the EEOC for sexual harassment was a protected activity, the Third Circuit opined that the actions which occurred after the complaint did not give rise to adverse employment action. Based upon this single retaliation in employment precedent, Judge Alito, given the opportunity, may have agreed with the dissent in *Jackson III*.

School Boards and Title IX

The *Jackson III* majority statement that school boards should have been on notice that retaliation under Title IX was actionable even prior to that decision is respectfully questioned. School boards across this nation are filled with hard-working individuals dedicated to education and equality of all students, but it is uncertain whether all school boards were aware before *Jackson III* that retaliation should be read into Title IX's implied private rights of actions. Now, however, school boards are on explicit notice that such behavior will not be tolerated.

Title IX's Legacy

Jackson v. Birmingham Board of Education (*Jackson III*) makes it clear that retaliation claims are now actionable under Title IX. Educational institutions receiving federal funds must now be even more diligent not to retaliate against an individual, male or female, who has complained about sex discrimination. Thus, Title IX's legacy, after thirty-four years, is still the pursuit of gender equity and the rights of those seeking gender equity in federally funded educational institutions.

Organizations to Contact

The editors have compiled the following list of organizations concerned with the issues debated in this book. The descriptions are derived from materials provided by the organizations. All have publications or information available for interested readers. The list was compiled on the date of publication of the present volume; the information provided here may change. Be aware that many organizations take several weeks or longer to respond to inquiries, so allow as much time as possible.

Association for Women's Rights in Development (AWID)
215 Spadina Ave., Suite 150
Toronto, ON   M5T 2C7 Canada
(416) 594-3773 • fax: (416) 594-0330
e-mail: contact@awid.org
Web site: www.awid.org

AWID is an international membership organization connecting, informing, and mobilizing people and groups committed to achieving gender equality, sustainable development, and women's human rights. The association's goal is to cause policy, institutional, and individual change that will improve the lives of women and girls. AWID is comprised of more than 5,000 women and men and is headquartered in Toronto. In addition to AWID's themed publications, which cover the areas of feminist movements and organizations, women's rights and economic change, young women and leadership, and gender equality and new technologies, the group also offers journals, handbooks, and materials exploring such topics as HIV/AIDS, globalization, and employment.

Center for Reproductive Rights
120 Wall St., New York, NY   10005
(917) 637-3600 • fax: (917) 637-3666
e-mail: info@reprorights.org
Web site: www.crlp.org

The Center for Reproductive Rights is a nonprofit legal advocacy organization dedicated to promoting and defending women's reproductive rights worldwide. Its Web site offers current legal news and medical information about legal advocacy, human rights, equality, safe pregnancies, contraception, and abortion, tailored to the laws of individual states and around the world. The center publishes numerous books, reports, and fact sheets promoting gender justice and the advancement of reproductive rights across the globe.

Legal Momentum
395 Hudson St., New York, NY   10014
(212) 925-6635 • fax: (212) 226-1066
e-mail: policy@legalmomentum.org
Web site: www.legalmomentum.org

Legal Momentum advances the rights of women and girls by using the power of the law to create innovative public policy. The organization has published *Women: A Celebration of Strength*, a book about women's accomplishments in education, work, family, culture, and community. The Web site offers online literature on child care, education, women's poverty, and legal resources.

MADRE
121 West 27th St., #301, New York, NY   10001
(212) 627-0444 • fax: (212) 675-3704
e-mail: madre@madre.org
Web site: www.madre.org

MADRE is an international women's human rights organization that works in partnership with community-based women's organizations worldwide to address issues of health and reproductive rights, economic development, education, and other human rights. Since its founding in 1983, MADRE has delivered over 22 million dollars worth of support to community-based women's organizations in Latin America, the Caribbean, the Middle East, Africa, Asia, the Balkans, and the United States. The group's Web site contains multiple press releases related to women's human rights and also compiles various articles concerning gender issues.

National Organization for Women (NOW)
1100 H Street NW, 3rd Fl., Washington, DC   20005
(202) 628-8669 • fax: (202) 785-8576
Web site: www.now.org

NOW is one of the largest and most well-known American organizations of feminist activists, with 500,000 contributing members and 550 chapters in all fifty states and the District of Columbia. It was founded in 1966 and seeks to eliminate discrimination and harassment of women in the workplace, schools, and the legal system. The group advocates for women's reproductive rights, including abortion and birth control. Among the association's official priorities are securing an amendment to the U.S. Constitution guaranteeing equal rights for women, ending racism and homophobia, and fighting the epidemic of violence against women. Through its Web site, NOW provides press releases, columns, and links to information and news on women's rights.

National Partnership for Women & Families
1875 Connecticut Avenue NW, Suite 650
Washington, DC   20009
(202) 986-2600 • fax: (202) 986-2539
email: info@nationalpartnership.org
Web site: www.nationalpartnership.org

The National Partnership for Women & Families is a nonprofit, nonpartisan organization that uses public education and advocacy to promote fairness in the workplace, quality health care, and policies that help women and men meet the dual demands of work and family. Working with business, government, unions, nonprofit organizations, and the media, the National Partnership strives to be a voice for fairness, a source for solutions, and a force for change. The organization's

Web site offers materials on such topics as the Family and Medical Leave Act, affirmative action, reproductive health, and workplace discrimination.

National Right to Life Committee
512 10th St. NW, Washington, DC 20004
(202) 626-8800
email: NRLC@nrlc.org
Web site: www.nrlc.org

The National Right to Life Committee is one of the largest organizations opposing abortion. It advocates a constitutional amendment granting embryos and fetuses the same right to life as those already born. The organization publishes a wealth of pro-life materials, including the brochure *Abortion in America* and the periodical *Right to Life News.*

Planned Parenthood Federation of America
434 West 33rd St., New York, NY 10001
(212) 541-7800
Web site: www.plannedparenthood.org

Planned Parenthood is the nation's leading sexual and reproductive health-care advocate and provider. The organization supports women's rights to make their own reproductive decisions without governmental interference. Planned Parenthood provides contraception, abortion, and family planning services at clinics nationwide. Among its extensive publications are the pamphlets *Abortions: Questions and Answers, Five Ways to Prevent Abortion,* and *Nine Reasons Why Abortions Are Legal.*

For Further Research

Books

Karen Blumenthal, *Let Me Play: The Story of Title IX, the Law That Changed the Future of Girls in America.* New York: Atheneum Books for Young Readers, 2005.

Angela Bonavoglia, *The Choices We Made: 25 Women and Men Speak Out About Abortion.* New York: Random House, 1991.

Susan Brownmiller, *In Our Time: Memoir of a Revolution.* New York: Dial, 1999.

Ruth Colker, *Abortion & Dialogue: Pro-Choice, Pro-Life, and American Law.* Bloomington: Indiana University Press, 1992.

Clare Cushman and Talbot D'Alemberte, *Supreme Court Decisions and Women's Rights: Milestones to Equality.* Washington, DC: CQ, 2001.

Eleanor Flexner and Ellen Fitzpatrick, *Century of Struggle: The Woman's Rights Movement in the United States.* Cambridge, MA: Belknap Press of Harvard University Press, 1996.

Jessica Gavora, *Tilting the Playing Field: Schools, Sports, Sex, and Title IX.* San Francisco: Encounter Books, 2002.

Maureen Harrison and Steve Gilbert, *Landmark Decisions of the United States Supreme Court.* Beverly Hills, CA: Excellent Books, 1991.

Catharine A. MacKinnon, *Sexual Harassment of Working Women: A Case of Sex Discrimination.* New Haven, CT: Yale University Press, 1979.

Jane J. Mansbridge, *Why We Lost the ERA*. Chicago: University of Chicago Press, 1986.

Susan Gluck Mezey, *Elusive Quality: Women's Rights, Public Policy, and the Law*. Boulder, CO: Lynne Rienner, 2003.

Danielle Nierenberg and Thomas Prugh, *Correcting Gender Myopia: Gender Equity, Women's Welfare, and the Environment*. Washington, DC: Worldwatch Institute, 2002.

Debran Rowland, *Boundaries of Her Body: A Troubling History of Women's Rights in America*. Naperville, IL: Sphinx, 2004.

Nadine Strossen, *Defending Pornography: Free Speech, Sex, and the Fight for Women's Rights*. New York: Scribner, 1995.

Sheila Tobias, *Faces of Feminism: An Activist's Reflections on the Women's Movement*. Boulder, CO: Westview, 1997.

Periodicals

Deborah J. Anderson, "Gender Equity in Intercollegiate Athletics: Determinants of Title IX Compliance," *Journal of Higher Education*, vol. 77, no. 2, March/April 2006.

Emily Bazelon, "Is There a Post-Abortion Syndrome?" *New York Times Magazine*, January 21, 2007.

Emily Tumbrink Brackstone, "Civil Rights: Title IX," *Tennessee Law Review*, vol. 73, Fall 2005.

Deborah Brake, "Revisiting Title IX's Feminist Legacy: Moving Beyond the Three-Part Test," *American University Journal of Gender, Social Policy & the Law*, vol. 12, 2004.

J. Shoshanna Ehrlich, "From Age of Consent Laws to the 'Silver Ring Thing': The Regulation of Adolescent Female Sexuality," *Health Matrix: Journal of Law-Medicine*, vol. 16, 2006.

Camille Fesche, "Title IX of the 1972 Education Amendments," *Georgetown Journal of Gender and the Law*, vol. 7, 2006.

Bill Finley, "Who's Afraid of Title IX?" *Sports Illustrated Women*, vol. 4, no. 8, December 2002–January 2003.

Garance Franke-Ruta, "Multiple Choice," *New Republic*, November 28–December 5, 2005.

Jennifer Frey, "Women's Team Leader," *Washington Post*, January 25, 2003.

John A. Gray, "Is Whistleblowing Protection Available under Title IX?: An Hermeneutical Divide and the Role of Courts," *William & Mary Journal of Women and the Law*, vol. 12, no. 3, Spring 2006.

Linda Greenhouse, "Justices Say Law on Sex Bias Guards Against Retaliation, Too," *New York Times*, March 30, 2005.

Donald P. Harris, Daniel B. Garrie, and Matthew J. Armstrong, "Sexual Harassment: Limiting the Affirmative Defense in the Digital Workplace," *University of Michigan Journal of Law Reform*, vol. 39, no. 1, Fall 2005.

Elizabeth A. Hoffmann, "Women Treated Differently: Why the 'Reasonable Woman' Standard Might Not Be Reasonable," *Equal Opportunities International*, vol. 23, nos. 3/4/5, 2004.

Margaret Moore Jackson, "A Half-Hearted Invitation: Welcoming Sexual Harassment in Minnesota," *William Mitchell Law Review*, vol. 33, no. 1, 2006.

Juliene James, "The Equal Pay Act in the Courts: A De Facto White-Collar Exemption," *New York University Law Review*, vol. 79, no. 5, November 2004.

Charisse Jones and Joan Biskupic, "Both Sides of Debate Predict More Procedure Restrictions," *USA TODAY*, April 19, 2007.

Linda Kalof, Kimberly K. Eby, Jennifer L. Matheson, and Rob J. Kroska, "The Influence of Race and Gender on Student Self-Reports of Sexual Harassment by College Professors," *Gender and Society*, vol. 15, no. 2, April 2001.

Maureen Kramlich, "The Abortion Debate Thirty Years Later: From Choice to Coercion," *Fordham Urban Law Journal*, vol. 31, no. 3, March 2004.

Charles Lane, "High Court Supports Title IX Protection," *Washington Post*, March 30, 2005.

Tecla Morasca, "Involuntary Childbirth and Prisoners' Rights: Court-Order Prison Policy Violates Fundamental Rights," *New England Journal on Criminal and Civil Confinement*, vol. 32, no. 1, Winter 2006.

Laura Oren, "Honor Thy Mother?: The Supreme Court's Jurisprudence of Motherhood," *Hastings Women's Law Journal*, vol. 17, 2006.

Katha Pollitt, "Prochoice Puritans," *Nation*, vol. 282, no. 6, February 13, 2006.

Ramesh Ponnuru, "Winning, and Losing, on Abortion—How Go the Wars?," *National Review*, May 8, 2006.

Beth A Quinn, "The Politics of Sexual Harassment: A Comparative Study of the United States, the European Union, and Germany," *Contemporary Sociology*, vol. 36, no. 3, May 2007.

Gretchen Reynolds, "See Jane Run," *Runner's World*, vol. 39, no. 11, November 2004.

Russell Shorto, "Contra-Contraception," *New York Times Magazine*, May 7, 2006.

Kenneth L. Thomas and Ramadanah M. Salaam, "The Face of Title IX: Post-*Jackson v. Birmingham Board of Education*," *Alabama Lawyer*, vol. 66, November 2005.

Robin Toner, "Abortion Foes See Validation for New Tactic," *New York Times*, May 22, 2007.

Christopher Uggen and Amy Blackstone, "Sexual Harassment as a Gendered Expression of Power," *American Sociological Review*, vol. 69, no. 1, February 2004.

Benjamin Wittes, "Letting Go of *Roe*," *Atlantic Monthly*, January/February 2005.

Index

sex discrimination in, 17–18, 156–157

See also Title IX

Education Amendments (1972), 17–18, 156

EEOC, Rogers v. (1971), 115

Eleventh Amendment, 101

Ellerth, Burlington Industries v. (1998), 146–149, 153–154

Ellison v. Brady (1991), 143–144

Employee Right to Choose Act, 107

Employer liability, in sexual harassment cases, 119–123, 131, 134–135, 144–150, 153–154

Enda, Jodi, 48

Ensoulment theory, 29

Epstein, Richard, 102

Equal Employment Opportunity Commission (EEOC), 120, 140, 153

Equal pay

history of laws on, 94–96

right to, 17

See also Wage inequities

Equal Pay Act (1963)

inadequacy of, 102–107

interpretation of, 96–97

passage of, 95–96

provisions of, 17

rulings on, 77–78, 80–92, 97–101

state employees and, 101–102

Equal Pay Matters Initiative, 106

Equality, for women, 45

F

Fair Labor Standards Act (FLSA), 95

Family-planning services, access to, 60–61

Faragher v. Boca Raton (1998), 146–149, 153–154

Feldt, Gloria, 57

Female sexuality, 42–43

Female workers, are paid less than men, 93–103

Feminists, concerns of, 14

Feminists For Life, 61

Ferguson, Plessy v. (1896), 70, 72

Fetuses

humanization of, 56–57, 62

personhood of, 21, 26–27

rights of, 29–30

Financial obstacles, to abortion, 36–37

Forklift Systems, Inc., Harris v. (1993), 141–142, 153

Forney, Georgette, 55–56

Foster, Serrin, 57

Fourteenth Amendment, 23, 26

France, 126

Freeman v. Pitts (1992), 72–73

G

Gandy, Kim, 54

Gender equity, under Title IX, 178–183

Ginsburg, Ruth Bader, 15, 16

Gonzales v. Carhart (2007), 14–17

Great Britain, 125

Green v. County School Board (1968), 70–71

Griswold v. Connecticut (1965), 20–21

H

Harris v. Forklift Systems, Inc. (1993), 141–142, 153

Hazen Paper Co. v. Biggins (1993), 170